CAMPFIRE CONFESSIONS

MORE TALES OF A
TEXAS GAME WARDEN

BENNY RICHARDS

CAMPFIRE CONFESSIONS
More Tales of a Texas Game Warden

©2022 Benny Richards

ISBN: 978-0-578-33124-9 (Paperback)
ISBN: 978-0-578-33125-6 (ePub)

Book design and layout: Lighthouse24

The stories in this book are true, firsthand accounts of events that occurred during my career. The people and places are real. However, in order to protect them and their families from further persecution and embarrassment, the names of suspects and violators have been changed.

As author of this book, I represent no one other than myself. The thoughts and opinions contained inside are mine alone.

About the Author

Benny Richards was born and raised in Hunt County, Texas. He spent his youth hunting, fishing, and picking up arrowheads in the fields and rivers in Northeast Texas. These experiences would serve him well as a Texas State Game Warden years later.

A graduate of East Texas State University in Commerce, Texas, Benny used his education to launch a career in law enforcement. He became a police officer in Richardson, Texas, in October 1993. After a short but successful tour of duty there, he entered the Texas Game Warden Training Center in Austin, Texas, on January 1, 1996.

His first duty assignment after graduation was in Delta County. During his game warden career, Benny was stationed in numerous counties, mostly in Northeast Texas, but he served all across Texas on different assignments. Benny received various awards and commendations throughout his career, including being named the Shikar Safari Wildlife Officer of the Year in 2015.

His love of storytelling led Benny to publish a weekly column called "Furry Tales" in his local newspaper. In addition to his reputation of being one of Texas's finest game wardens, Benny is probably best known for his role in the popular TV show *Lone Star Law* that aired on Animal Planet. Benny makes his home now near the small community of Campbell, Texas.

*This book was written in honor of my father
who taught me how to be a man*

*and my mother
who taught me how to be a better man.*

A local rancher called the game warden in Navasota
To report a poacher that made his escape in a black Toyota.

That very same morning with a promise not to fail
The warden gathered the evidence and got hot on the trail.

Stopping behind a big red barn to continue his investigation
The warden stepped inside without any hesitation

Once inside he discovered what he was after
A white-tail doe was swinging from a rafter.

A few feet away stood a man with a knife
Of course, he knew nothing about the deer, he swore on his life.

The man's explanation didn't pass the legal test
So he quickly found himself placed under arrest.

Arriving at the jail at noon, the man asked wryly,
"What's for dinner?"
The warden just laughed and said, "Nothing for you my friend...
'Cause you are a sinner!"

CONTENTS

PREFACE

THE FIRST TIME I EVER REMEMBER seeing a game warden was sometime around the spring of 1975. At that time, my family was living south of the little town of Wolfe City, Texas. One sunny morning with nothing better to do, my brother and I walked down to the Highway 34 bridge that crossed over Honey Creek. At the bridge, we sat on the guard railing and began plinking at frogs, turtles, rocks, or whatever else made a good target. I was equipped with an old single-shot .22 rifle, my brother had his trusty Crosman BB gun. Suddenly, a big, long, silver car stopped in the center of the bridge a few feet from us. I still remember that sick feeling I had when I gazed upon that big, baby-blue emblem on the side of the door.

The driver's side window slowly rolled down. A big, burly man inside, wearing a brown uniform, asked, "What are you boys shooting at?"

Afraid that we were in trouble, I answered, "Just turtles."

He just grinned and replied, "Y'all don't be shooting off the bridge." He then rolled up the window and drove away.

My brother and I scurried off the bridge at once. I had finally seen one, and at the age of fourteen, I was impressed by game wardens. Before that day, I had only heard stories about them. As a younger boy, I remember sitting around the big table at deer camp listening to stories about wardens from my dad, my uncles, and their hunting buddies. At that age, when you hear stories about a thing but never see one, that thing kinda becomes a mythical being. For a long time, that's what game wardens were to me, mythical beings that you had to constantly be on the lookout for anytime you were hunting or fishing.

After that spring day in 1975, I spent countless thousands of hours in the woods and along the creeks pursuing wild game of every sort. I never had any other contact with wardens for almost twenty-five years. Little did I know at the time, but all those hours spent in duck blinds, tree stands, and boats was on-the-job training for a long career that was coming.

I graduated high school in May of 1980, and through a stroke of luck fell into a summer job with Mobil Oil Corporation doing seismographic oil exploration in Wyoming. When I flew up to Wyoming to start work, I thought I had died and gone to Heaven. It was the first time I had laid my eyes on the Rocky Mountains. Living and working in those mountains surrounded by all that breathtaking beauty and wildlife was one of the best times of my life. Here again, I didn't realize it at the time but it was more on-the-job training for what was coming.

In August of 1980, I packed my bags and left the mountains and traveled to Lubbock, Texas, where I enrolled at Lubbock Christian College. I had signed a letter of intent to play college football there. I wished I could say I enjoyed my time at LCC, but I really can't. Football was fun, but I didn't like Lubbock and didn't really fit in at the school. Part of my problem was I missed Wyoming and I was homesick for my little hometown at the same time. Leaving Lubbock behind, I went back and enrolled in East Texas State University in Commerce, Texas. Over the following three years, I bounced back and forth between Texas and Wyoming before finally throwing the towel in on college altogether.

In October of 1983, I packed everything I owned into my old 1964 Chevy pickup truck and headed for Gillette, Wyoming. I had decided to make seismograph work with Mobil Oil a full-time gig. For the next twelve months, the crew I was working with traveled a lot. We put in stints in Kansas, Colorado, Wyoming, and finally Montana. Life was grand and I was having a ball until one day I got the rug jerked out from underneath me. At that time, a barrel of oil was worth about fourteen dollars a barrel. I don't know for sure, but I guess the company I worked for figured they could buy oil overseas a lot cheaper than they search for it in the good ole USA. Anyway, Mobil Oil shut our crew down and sent us all home. I found myself back in Texas, unemployed and without any direction in my life. I came close to joining the Marine Corps at one point but backed out. I got back into college part time and eventually landed a job with a good company in Greenville, Texas.

In April of 1986, I went to work at Case International. Even though it was a job in a big, dusty warehouse, it paid well. During my time at Case, I met my future wife, Kristi, in a college class we had together. A little over a year later, we were married. Another year passed, and our first child arrived. Even though I didn't like my job, all the bills were paid and life was pretty good. Now the rug got jerked out from under me a second time.

One day, totally unexpected, a group of men wearing suits and carrying briefcases came to Greenville from the home office in Racine, Wisconsin. They were at our warehouse to tell over one hundred people, including me, that we were all now unemployed. Being laid off without a job and with a wife and a baby at home scared me to death, but I must admit I almost felt relieved. No one will ever know how badly I hated that job. I did not look back when I walked out the door. I didn't let any grass grow under my feet before I was on the move. Loved ones were counting on me and I had no time to spare.

The very next day, I was back in college full time. I was close to getting my degree and I knew if I didn't finish now I never would. At this point in my life, things were set into motion with an eventual result that could have only been planned by the good Lord Himself. I can't say enough about how my parents and in-laws helped Kristi and me during this time. Over the next two years, as I completed my degree, I had a lot of time to do some serious soul-searching. I needed to figure out what I wanted to do with my life. I was definitely not the kind of person that could punch a time clock every day. When I thought about what I was really good at, what skills I had to offer, and what I liked to do, one career jumped out at me. GAME WARDEN! I made the decision to put all my efforts in that direction. Although I would eventually be successful, there were some tall hurdles left to clear.

I applied for the forty-third Game Warden Training Academy in the spring of 1992. I went through the hiring process with a lot of confidence and advanced every step, all the way to the final interview in Austin. I thought I was a sure bet for a spot but I guess the powers that be at the academy had other ideas. I got a "no thanks, try again" letter in the mail. I was crushed and a little angry, especially when I found out who some of the people were who had been offered a position ahead of me.

There was no time to feel sorry for myself. A few weeks later I was on my way to Richardson, Texas, to apply for one of four open police officer positions there. When I walked into the convention center where the entrance exam was being given to all the applicants, I stopped in my tracks at the front door. Over four hundred men and women were there, all competing for the same four slots. I came so close to just going back home. Then I found out that five extra points were to be given to all veterans.... I was no veteran. With this many people, I figured the odds against me were great. However, I stayed and took the exam anyway. I'm glad I did.

The following week, I got a call from the recruitment officer with the Richardson Police Department. She advised me that I was number sixteen on the hire list. That didn't sound all that great to me until she explained that I was actually in a very good position due to the fact that so many applicants would fail the background check. To make a long story short, I was the very first of four other successful applicants to be offered a job. I started the police academy in May of 1993 and eventually graduated as class salutatorian. My law enforcement career had begun. After hitting the streets, it didn't take long for me to figure out that law enforcement was the business I needed to be in. The brass also noticed quickly that I was a damn good cop. My time on the force at Richardson gave me the opportunity to deal with every kind of crook, dope head, and con artist imaginable. It was good training for later.

In the spring of 1995, I was in a good position to start moving up through the ranks at the PD. At that very same time, the Game Warden Academy began taking applications for their forty-fourth cadet class. I threw my name back in the hat along with over 2,500 other people. I went through their hiring process all over again, but it was a little different this go around. I had a chip on my shoulder from being turned down two years earlier. During interviews, I didn't care what anyone thought about me or my answers and I would have gladly stayed at the PD if it had come to that. I actually think my "this is your last chance to get me" attitude actually helped me during that final interview.

After the final interview was complete, all the applicants were gathered up at the track at a local high school to complete the physical assessment test. The physical assessment included push-ups, sit-ups, flexibility tests, and a mile-and-a-half run. Before each test, I began to notice several of the applicants who were waiting their turn kept asking the coordinator, "How many do I have to do to pass?" I thought to myself, "How stupid is that?" Why not do as many as you possibly could and not worry about it? Just before the mile-and-a-half run, many applicants were all basically asking, "How slowly can I run this and still pass?" The coordinator advised, "Sixteen minutes." Are you kidding me? I could have crawled a mile and a half on my hands and knees in sixteen minutes. I knew right then some of these folks were just plain lazy and cared only about doing just enough, instead of pushing themselves physically. The bad thing was some of these lazy humans were going to become game wardens. I made up my mind that I was going to use every bit of energy I could muster and make these six laps around this track as fast as I physically could.

At the word go, I started running. After lapping most everyone in the pack at least once, I rounded the last curve and headed for the finish line. I wasn't in the greatest shape at the time and my lungs felt like they were going to explode. As I crossed the finish in just under nine minutes, I walked to the side of the track and collapsed in the grass infield. As I lay there trying to catch my breath, I saw Lieutenant Cinda Brooks, the training coordinator, approaching. She walked up and said, "That was a good run." Unable to speak, I just nodded my head. She wrote something down on her clipboard and walked away.

The forty-fourth Game Warden Cadet Class started on January 1, 1996, in Austin, Texas. My name was on the roster. I had made it. Over the next seven and a half months, I used my extensive outdoor experience, police training, and physical abilities to excel. On July 31 of that year, my classmates and our families gathered at the state capitol for graduation. I graduated at the top of my class and was assigned to Delta County in northeast Texas.

One month later, Kristi, Kaitlin, Erik, and I showed up in Cooper, Texas, and my great game warden adventure began.

Toys In The Attic

I WAS LOADING EQUIPMENT into my patrol truck when Kevin Davis pulled up into my driveway. He had dropped in to say goodbye. Kevin had recently transferred to the department's environ-mental crime unit, which meant he would be relocating to the Dallas area.

"Hey, gentle Ben, do you wanna go grab some lunch before I leave town?"

I said, "Sure, that sounds great.... But first, since you are here, I need you to go help me with something."

He replied, "Ok, then, whatcha got?"

"I've got a felony warrant on a guy that I need to serve."

I actually had two arrest warrants for a subject named Bradlie Don Snow. A week earlier, I had witnessed Snow use a six-inch knife to stab another man. When I attempted to arrest him for the violent assault, he fled in a vehicle. He ended up crashing the vehicle a short distance away but escaped on foot. A judge in Hunt County issued warrants the very next day. I had done some digging, trying to locate Snow, who was basically a freeloading vagrant. I finally uncovered some information that he was shacked up with a woman. With an address in hand, Kevin and I headed to Commerce, Texas. The location we were traveling to was an area of town known locally as "Green Acres." It was a bunch of government-owned duplex apartments for low-income families. As we arrived and pulled into the big parking lot, I was on high alert. Snow was dangerous and he was a runner. Parking in front of unit 6B, I radioed the local police department dispatch, gave them our location, and asked them to send an extra officer. Kevin and I exited the truck and I walked to the front door of the apartment as Kevin walked around to cover the back door. I knocked loudly and got no response. I checked the knob and found the door to be locked. I knocked again more forcefully and shouted, "Police!" Again, there was no response from within the apartment. My thoughts at this point were, "Well, damn, I really wanted to get this guy and wrap this up." Not knowing if the apartment was occupied, and with few options, I walked around to where Kevin was posted. After a brief discussion, we decided to just leave and come back after lunch. As we were getting back into the patrol truck, we were approached by a man that turned out to be the apartment maintenance man.

He inquired, "Are y'all looking for Brad?"

I assumed he was referring to Bradlie Snow, so I said, "Yes, we are." The man advised, "He is in the apartment."

"Are you absolutely sure he is in there?"

"Yes, he is in there.... He was smoking a cigarette on the front porch and ran inside when y'all pulled up."

This changed everything. The maintenance man went on to explain that Snow had been given a trespass warning and wasn't supposed to be on the property. I confirmed this info with local police. A few minutes later, a half dozen officers showed up. They were all familiar with our fugitive and wanted his ass as bad as I did. More knocking on the front door produced no results. Then, our maintenance guy came through with a master key. Unlocking the front door revealed the door was also restrained by a chained lock on the inside. Again, the helpful maintenance man came through a second time.

"I can take the door off at the hinges if y'all want me to."

After a conference with the police, that plan was implemented. As Kevin and I stood back and watched, the front door was removed and in rushed the local officers. After a few minutes of waiting, I expected to see Snow being escorted out in handcuffs. Instead, an officer came out and said, "He ain't in there."

"Say what?"

I pointed out that the door had been chained from the inside.... He had to be inside.... Or someone had to be inside. The officer just shrugged his shoulders and said, "We have looked everywhere."

"Come on, Kevin, let's go get this guy."

Kevin and I entered the apartment and began to conduct our own search of the premises. After a thorough search, we were unable to find anyone in the apartment either. Frustrated, I just stood silently in the kitchen and began to think. It was at that moment that I looked down a long hallway and noticed something. The attic access door. It was just ever so slightly ajar and there was a small piece of insulation hanging out of a crack between the door and the molding.

"Hey, Kevin, come here."

"Did you find something?"

"Yeah, I think I did."

Pointing up at the attic access door, I smiled, which brought a similar smile to Kevin's face. After retrieving a chair from the kitchen, I stood on it to reach up and pull down the access door. Snow must have had some monkey in him to be able to get up in that attic without aid of a chair or ladder. After crawling up into the dark attic, I used my flashlight to search for him. I took a really stupid chance getting up in that confined space unprotected. Snow was a very violent human and he could have had a gun or other weapon. If he had been armed with a gun, I would have been a sitting duck. Back in those days, I was a risk taker. It's a miracle I lived through those dangerous decisions. Anyway, working clockwise, I slowly examined the attic space. I saw nothing at first, just some children's toys stored in boxes. But then, I saw it. Because it was a duplex, the apartment shared a common attic with the next apartment, the two sides separated by a layer of sheetrock. I could clearly see a large hole had been kicked through the sheetrock. I knew then he was up there.

I leaned down and told Kevin and the other officers about what I was observing. I told him and the other officers to stay put as I crawled through the hole to the other side. Once on the other side, I drew my pistol and stood motionless as I looked for Snow. I was in disbelief when I did not see any signs of him. Taking a closer second look, I saw something out of place few feet away...a lump in the insulation. A closer inspection startled me. It was him. He was lying flat between two rafters. He had covered himself almost completely with the loose insulation. The only things visible were his toes, hands, and face. I noticed his eyes were closed and he was unaware that I had seen him.

Reholstering my pistol, I turned and leaned through the hole in the sheetrock. I motioned for Kevin to join me. He asked the officers below to stand by. Standing on either side and speaking through the hole in the sheetrock, I whispered to Kevin and briefed him on the situation. I then helped him to crawl through the hole. Slowly and carefully, walking on rafters, Kevin and I surrounded him. I stood two feet behind his head...Kevin just below his feet. Suddenly, Snow's eyes opened and he sat straight up. Kevin and I pounced upon him. He started to struggle, which caused me to yell at the top of my lungs, "I am a state game warden and you are under arrest!" My words after that were the standard ass chewing I administered to all lawbreakers under similar conditions. Kevin and I made quick work of handcuffing our suspect. However, this ordeal wasn't quite over.

Kevin and I were startled when we heard a loud crashing sound behind us. We spun around just in time to see an officer disappear between two rafters, through the sheetrock, headed south down to the living room floor below. After hearing all the commotion our arrest caused, the officer had assumed we needed assistance. He was coming to our aid. The problem was he didn't understand construction principles like…a 220-pound man cannot run across a sheetrock ceiling. The sheetrock gave way and through the ceiling he went. Miraculously, he was unharmed during the fall, only embarrassed.

We completed our arrest and removed Snow from the attic. Commerce officers took him into custody and whisked him off to jail. The real hero in this whole episode turned out to be the reliable maintenance man. He repaired the ceiling in the apartment before the occupants returned home. That arrest was the last opportunity I ever had to work with Kevin. I did my best to give him a good send-off.

VANISHED

"HEY, MAN, WE NEED your help on something."

"Whatcha got?"

"Well, we can't really figure it out yet. A man is missing up here near Celeste but we have turned his place upside down and can't find him. The DPS helicopter is here and the prison tracking dogs, too."

"When was the last time he was seen?"

"Earlier today he was working on his property using a skid steer...then he just vanished."

"Who reported him missing?"

"His family did."

I told the deputy I would be there in thirty minutes then hung up the phone. On the short drive to the rural farm in northern Hunt County, I tried to come up with a scenario in which someone goes missing on their own property. Without any more information than I got over the phone, I could come up with nothing. It was dark when I arrived about nine o'clock. Driving through the front gate, I watched as the DPS helicopter flew over my head and headed west. I assumed it was leaving and headed back to Garland, Texas. I pulled up to several patrol cars and parked near a fence line where I was greeted by the deputy. A few yards away, I observed horses and dogs being loaded onto a trailer.

"Have y'all found him yet?"

14

"No, sir we haven't. The helicopter just left and the prison guys said their dogs haven't hit on anything. They are leaving, too."

At this point I asked the deputy to fill in the blanks for me.

"How old is this man?'

"In his seventies, I believe."

"How large is his place?"

"About a hundred acres."

He went on to explain the man, along with the skid steer he was driving, hadn't been seen in over nine hours. I asked the obvious questions.

"Has someone walked the perimeter and looked for any breaks in his fence line? Has someone looked for tracks at the end of the driveway leading off the property? Did someone try to call his cell phone?"

Yes, yes, and yes. None of what I was hearing was making any sense to me. I would have thought someone was pulling a practical joke if it wasn't very obvious that the situation was very real. How can a man in his seventies, driving an eleven-thousand-pound piece of construction equipment, disappear on one hundred acres of land in a way that helicopters and tracking dogs could not find him? I asked the deputy to take me to the man's family. He led me to the house not far away and introduced me to the missing man's adult son. After introducing myself, I asked the man to tell me about the last time anyone had seen his father. He explained that his father had been doing some dirt work near a pond by the barn. At noon, the family told their dad lunch was ready and to come in and eat. He said he would be in shortly. That was the last time anyone saw him. A terrible thought suddenly entered my mind. I asked the son to take me to the area where his father had been working earlier. Using my flashlight, we crossed a fence and walked around the barn and fifty more yards to the spot. Standing on a berm overlooking the pond, I could see fresh equipment tracks in the disturbed dirt near the shoreline.

"Are there any more ponds on the property?"

"Yes, one more back in the woods."

Now my hunch was becoming a credible theory. I pulled the deputy to the side and told him to find the other pond in the woods and check it out. He left immediately. Now, turning my attention back to the son, I asked, "Do you have a pole or something long I could use? I want to check something."

"Yes, I'll be right back."

He returned with a ten-foot piece of PVC pipe. As he handed it to me, I could see the concern building on his face. I walked to the edge of the pond and slowly began to probe around the shoreline. It didn't take long. Suddenly, I was tapping on something very hard submerged five feet below the surface.

"Do you know of anything large that is supposed to be in this pond?"

"No."

"Then go get help."

I shucked my gun belt and dove into the pond. The skid steer the man had been driving had an enclosed glass cab. Was there any chance he was still alive inside the cab nine hours later? Almost 100 percent NO but I needed to prove it to myself. Without the ability to see, I had to use my sense of touch. Using my hands and feet, I determined the cab door was shut, but after several attempts, I was unable to open the door. The fate of the man inside was unknown with any certainty. As I waded out of the muddy water back onto shore, all the first responders were arriving. Hunt County Constable Terry Jones had already ordered a wrecker to the scene. Absolutely nothing could be done now but wait. By this time, all the family members in the house had been notified of what was going on. It was gut wrenching to hear the pain in their voices as they grasped what had happened. It was notable that, even in their pain, they were gracious and helpful during the entire event.

When the wrecker arrived, it was backed into position at the edge of the pond just above where the skid steer was resting on the bottom. I swam back out into the pond and found a spot where I could actually stand on the submerged machine with my head out of water. I was given the winch cable and was able to secure it to a blade arm. I swam to the center of the pond and treaded water as the winch on the wrecker tightened. More and more pressure on the cable caused it to snap in half. The recoiling cable knocked out the back windshield of the wrecker. The extremely heavy skid steer was lodged in the thick mud at the bottom of the pond. It became obvious that one wrecker would not be enough. Two more wreckers were summoned to the scene. Working in concert with each other, the two wreckers were able to pull the machine out of the pond and onto the shoreline in just under an hour. Once it was removed, the grim reality was revealed. The man had passed on to another life. A sad, sad tale indeed.

WEEDS

THE OPENING DAY OF DOVE SEASON in 1999 started like any other but it certainly didn't end like any other before it for me. That September afternoon near Cooper, I was backed up in a tree line waiting for someone to come along and shoot a bird off the high lines in front of me. I had the seat leaned back and was listening to the radio when I got a call from my captain, Skip McBride. He was talking fast and I could tell there was some urgency in his voice. Skip told me to head to Morris County as fast as I could get there and find game wardens Billy Dodd and Shawn Hervey. He didn't give many details but evidently Billy and Shawn had stumbled onto some sort of dope growing operation and had armed men running from them in the woods. This sounded like a hell of a deal that I didn't want to miss. I pointed my patrol truck south and punched it.

As I was flying down FM 71 near Sugar Hill, I finally got Shawn on his cell phone. Shawn, who was a very excitable type of guy, began yelling something about Billy firing a shot and "Mexicans" with guns running through the woods. He was so excited and out of breath I didn't get much out of the conversation before he hung up. I then called Billy, who was the exact opposite personality of Shawn. Slowly speaking into the phone as if it was just another day at the office, Billy explained he was deep in the woods on the White Oak Wildlife Management Area. He went on to say there was marijuana growing everywhere. He didn't have to tell me to hurry as I closed the flip phone and stuck it in my pocket.

The northern part of Morris County where I was headed was locally known as Twin Lakes. It was thousands of acres of public hunting land dissected by the Sulphur River on one side and White Oak Creek on the other. This area was the closest thing to a jungle in the State of Texas. I left the interstate and drove a couple of miles down the county road that led to Twin Lakes. I then came to a roadblock that was manned by two state troopers. I got out and briefly spoke to the troopers, who had the latest information. I was advised that Billy, Shawn, and two DPS narcotics officers had located a huge marijuana growing operation that was occupied by six to seven individuals who had fled into the woods. One of the individuals was reported to be carrying an AK-47. One shot had been fired near a large bamboo hut and all the suspects were still at large. In deciding what to do next, I fell back on my common sense and knowledge of the public hunting area. It was very hot...probably 95 degrees in the shade on that day. I was told that some of the runners fled barefooted when Billy scattered them. I concluded the only real chance for escape would be to find the Sulphur River and follow it north to the interstate. At the highway they would call for, flag down, or hijack a ride.

I mounted up and went back to the interstate and drove to the long bridge that crossed the Sulphur River. There was a deputy sitting in his squad car on the bridge. Two other squad cars were slowly driving on the shoulder along the interstate. I thought to myself, "Damn, do game wardens have to figure out everything?" I guess all these deputies thought the bad guys would see them, run out of the woods and surrender, and confess to felony crimes. It took me about five minutes to round everyone up for a roadside meeting. I asked all them to stay out of sight until dark. I collected a few cell phone numbers and then explained I was going in on foot. They all looked at me like I was crazy but agreed to the plan.

I hid my patrol truck in a large group of pines in the center median about three hundred yards from the bridge. Grabbing my Ruger Mini-14 rifle, I bailed out and ran down the side of the interstate to a spot where I crawled over the fence near the river. When I entered the woods, sweat was pouring down my face. The underbrush was thick in front of me as I made my way along the riverbank. About two hundred yards in, I found a slight clearing where I could see anything moving in any direction. I got behind a huge oak tree and sat down. As I sat silently watching and listening, I felt confident I was in a good spot. The more I ran scenarios through my head the more convinced I was that I would catch the runners coming through the woods. Little did I know how close I was to a big surprise that would not reveal itself until the next day.

I never saw anything as I slapped mosquitos off my face until it was too dark to see. Disappointed, I finally gave up the chase and made my way back to my truck. The bad guys made their escape and were not located. Even though it was nighttime now, the day wasn't even close to being over. All the officers involved met at the front gate to decide how to proceed. Captain McBride had arrived, along with wardens Larry Rowe, Kenneth Hand, and Jerry Ash. The two DPS officers that where involved in the discovery of the illicit operation were ordered by their superiors to spend the night protecting the area in case the illegal farmers showed back up. Captain McBride directed all the wardens to transport the two officers back into the remote area on four-wheelers and give them any support they needed through the night.

Getting from the front gate back to the grow was not easy during the daylight. At night, it was almost impossible. There were snakes, spiders, and vicious mosquitos to contend with. Thorns, nettles, and briars were constantly sticking and cutting your skin. Attempting to navigate the creeks, sloughs, and mudholes in the dark kept you turning in circles. In spite of it all, Billy led us all back to the big bamboo hut surrounded by marijuana about midnight. When I finally laid my eyes on the hut where the men had been living, I was amazed. It had been constructed by digging a shallow two-foot pit in the ground. Around the pit, a wooden frame had been built using saplings. The whole thing was then covered using cane that grew in abundance near the river. Inside, we discovered sleeping bags, propane bottles, a small cookstove, lanterns, handgun ammo, and unfortunately for the bad guys...a cell phone.

As warden Shawn Hervey and I were using flashlights to inspect the interior of the hut, I spied a souvenir. There was a Mexican flag featuring Our Lady of Guadalupe hanging from the ceiling. These definitely were not local boys. Outside the hut, we found three deer heads hanging in a tree. Evidently, they had a taste for venison. Surrounding the hut were three acres of growing marijuana six feet tall. Believe me when I tell you that a lot of marijuana can be grown on three acres. All through the growing plants was an elaborate watering system made of garden hoses. Water to feed the crop was pulled out of the Sulphur River using small gasoline-powered water pumps. After an hour of searching the area in the dark, I was still trying to comprehend what I was seeing. This was a sight I thought belonged down in some South American jungle....not East Texas. After dropping off the narcotics officers along with food and bottled water, all the wardens left, vowing to be back at first light. The trip out was just as challenging as the trip in.

When the sun came back up, I left the house and drove back to our staging area on the public hunting area. All the same wardens had shown back up, along with a small army of deputies and DEA agents. We all saddled up on four-wheelers and made our way back to the dope fields in a long line. The two DPS guys that had spent the night guarding the area met us with horror stories of the mosquito attacks they had endured overnight. Everyone went to work dismantling the grow operation. DEA agents began cutting down the plants with machetes and transporting everything out one load at a time. Deputies were busy photographing everything. Game wardens all fanned out and continued to search the area. Warden Larry Rowe and I made an interesting discovery not too far away. A small rope we located lying on the ground turned out to be tied to a small frame made of branches and covered with leaves. Pulling on the rope raised the frame and exposed a large pit in the ground filled with garbage. We eventually uncovered many more garbage pits.

The hard, sweaty work continued throughout the morning. Just before noon, a DPS helicopter showed up and began flying over the area high overhead. Flying in ever widening circles, the chopper searched until it reached an area on the banks of the Sulphur River. At this point, we all observed it begin to hoover in one spot just above the trees. The pilot stated over the radio that they had discovered another big field of growing marijuana. He further advised that the best way to reach it would be to go in on foot from the interstate highway. Upon hearing this, Larry, Shawn, and I scrambled back out to our trucks and headed around to the Interstate 30 river bridge. Parking under the bridge, we all grabbed our rifles and hit the woods. Shawn moved along the river as Larry and I flanked him on the right. We passed right through the area where I had sat until dark the previous afternoon. Three hundred yards into the thick timber, Larry and I froze when we heard Shawn barking out commands to "come out with your hands up!"

"He's got something Larry…. Let's go." I took off running through the trees toward the sound of Shawn's voice. Suddenly, I realized I was running through growing marijuana two feet taller than my head. Shawn was still yelling as I came through the stalks with Larry right behind me. When I saw what he was yelling at, I went down to one knee and threw up my rifle, ready for a fight. Fifty feet in front of us was another hut. A much larger and more elaborate one than found the previous day. Beside it was a clothesline with several pairs of jeans and a couple of shirts hanging.

"Shawn do you see anyone in there?"

"I don't know."

A few tense seconds went by before we slowly, carefully made our way to the small, circular entrance to the hut. The hut turned out to be empty. My hair was still standing on end when I looked around and saw all the human footprints in the soft dirt. Whoever was here last was barefooted. After calling for more officers, Shawn, Larry, and I spread out and took up positions. We sat silently as the helicopter circled above, unaware if we were being watched. Thirty minutes passed before deputies began to show up. When they did, they told us that on their way in they had found a large duffle bag filled with marijuana. As it turned out, the duffle of dope was hidden at the exact spot where I had crossed the fence the previous afternoon. Obviously, the armed men who had run away from Billy did not immediately leave the area. They instead hid until after darkness and spent the night trying to salvage what they could of their crop before exiting for good. Who knows why they left the big duffle bag behind? Perhaps they had more dope than they could carry out to a waiting vehicle.

When more deputies began arriving, I set out on foot, walking a straight line back to the original hut. I was beginning to realize this operation was much larger than anything we could have imagined. The distance between the two huts was about a quarter mile as a crow would fly. As I followed a well- worn trail through the thick underbrush, I found another cell phone lying on the ground in front of me. Walking a little farther, I found a machete. I continued up the trail with my rifle at the ready. The next thing I know, I'm standing in what could only be described as a village. To my left was a pavilion type structure. To my right was another hut just like the first two. Through the woods in front of me, I could see other small structures. Everything was covered in cane. I just sat motionless for a few seconds. Without hearing any sounds or seeing any movement, I decided the bad guys were all gone. Everything had indeed been abandoned. I turned around and hauled ass back down the trail to report what I had found. When I returned with everyone, they were all amazed. The large pavilion turned out to be where all the cut marijuana was dried before being cut and packaged in the hut only a few yards away. One of the other small structures was actually a well-stocked kitchen. It would be hard to determine how many men this grow operation actually supported.

This was the day my eyes were opened to the reality of what was really going on in my own country. The truth was the drug wars had come to the heart of America. Whoever was behind this operation spared no expense and they were brazen to attempt to pull this off in the backyard of small-town USA. The DEA and DPS brought in more agents as the size and scope of it all became clearer. We spent the rest of that day dismantling the village and collecting evidence in one-hundred-degree heat. I don't ever remember sweating like that before or since. There were two things discovered that day that were of interest to me. Lifejackets were found inside the third hut. I think boats were used initially to haul in all the equipment in the early spring when the water was up in the river and nearby sloughs. The second thing was a small structure that Larry found built on the riverbank at a bend in the river. It was circular in shape and just large enough for one man to squeeze into. A small window was cut into the side in order for someone to look out over the river. A wooden "rest" was built just below the window. We all decided the structure was a guardhouse used to watch for anyone approaching from the river. The "rest" was built to steady a rifle in case a shot was needed. These people were dangerous whoever they were.

When the sun came up on the third day, Billy and I were launching our flat-bottomed boats into the Sulphur River south of the interstate bridge. We made the short trip upriver to where wardens and DEA agents were busy cutting down the remaining marijuana. After being cut down, the stalks were tied into large bundles and thrown off the riverbank down to our waiting boats below. Billy and I loaded everything into our boats and hauled it back to the bridge. The process required twelve trips. At the bridge, agents loaded the dope onto trailers where it would be taken back to a law enforcement storage facility in Dallas. It was estimated that over twelve thousand marijuana plants were removed. The dollar value of harvested and unharvested dope was in the millions. DPS took over the investigation after the village was totally dismantled and burnt. I was told later that agents used the cell phones that were recovered and a small notebook that was found to develop several suspects. In addition, the serial numbers off of water pumps left behind were used to identify a credit card that purchased those pumps at a farm store in Addison, Texas. The credit card supposedly belonged to someone living in a million-dollar mansion in North Dallas. Go figure that. It all just goes to show that wild animals are not the only thing lurking in the woods of East Texas anymore.

Tarzan I Am Not

THERE WAS NOTHING I HATED WORSE than losing a good deer, so I just couldn't lose this one. After shooting a big ten-point buck near the Sulphur River, I sat down next to a tall pin oak tree to wait five minutes before following him into the thicket where I last saw him. I had hit him hard in the sweet spot with a .270. I watched him buck like a horse when the bullet passed through. Fifty yards at most. That's as far as I thought he would run before his oil light came on. I got up and slowly walked over to the edge of the thicket and immediately found a blood trail. After swinging my rifle over my right shoulder, I got in line and began to follow the trail into the heavy timber. Fifty yards later, I was still following drops of blood in front of me but they were becoming sparse. At seventy-five yards the blood trail stopped at the edge of a slough. I could clearly see muddy hoof prints exiting the slough on the opposite side. At this point, I decided to give the buck some more time to kick the bucket before following any farther.

I drove back to my home and grabbed a bite to eat before heading back. I was beginning to get a bad feeling as I grabbed two flashlights and headed back to the river. Just over two hours had passed and it was now pitch black as I went back into the woods. I searched high and low until both flashlights gave out on me without finding another single drop of blood. I was sick with disappointment. I finally gave up and went back home empty-handed. It was hard getting to sleep that night as I kept replaying the whole thing over and over in my head. I began to question whether I had made a good shot after all.

The next morning, I was sitting at the kitchen table eating breakfast when Kristi told me she needed to run to the store in Sulphur Springs to pick up some groceries. With the previous afternoon's events still in my head, I decided I needed to give it one more try before giving up on my buck. I asked Kristi if she would drop me off at the woods on her way to town and pick me up on her way back. It was a good plan. As I got out of the car on the side of the narrow highway, Kristi said she would pick me up back here at the bridge at eleven o'clock. She then drove away. I walked into the woods less than enthusiastic. I made my way back to the big slough and at that spot began to walk in large circles hoping to find signs.

I was on my third loop when I found blood smeared on the side of a sapling. Looking to the east, I could see a dim trail leading through a group of cedar trees. Following the trail, I rounded a corner and came face-to-face with the wounded buck. He was bedded down at the base of a small tree only thirty feet away. I could clearly see dried blood around a wound to his shoulder. The whole thing would have been over right then right there if it was not for one big problem. I didn't bring a gun with me. What a stupid mistake. Standing as still as I could, I glanced down at my wristwatch. The hands on the watch delivered the news. It would be forty-five minutes before Kristi would be back. Without a clue what else to do, I slowly lowered myself to the ground. The buck's eyes were trained on my every move but he made no attempt to get up off the ground. A long staring contest began now. I wondered if he was too injured to move. I thought if I stayed quiet and still, I could watch him until Kristi returned. When she got back, I planned on easing back out of the woods and going home to get my rifle.

The minutes passed slowly. The cold stares continued until 10:55. With only five minutes to go until Kristi was due to return, I decided it was time to make a move. As I slowly stood up, the buck surprised me by standing up also. I froze and hoped he would relax and lie back down. He did not. The buck stretched and then began limping away from me. I was in panic mode now. My mind was racing as I tried to decide what to do. One thing was for certain. He was not bleeding any longer and if he kept going, I would never find him again. If I was going to put my tag on this buck, I needed to do something now...right now. But what? Just then I remembered the folding pocketknife I always carried. Without hesitation I pulled the knife out of my pants pocket and opened it. Holding the knife with the blade pointing down from my fist, I charged the buck. This was something right out of a Tarzan movie but I was determined to kill this deer. The sound of me crushing leaves behind him caused the buck to quicken his pace. I was right behind him dodging trees and jumping over logs. The faster I ran, the faster he ran. This went on for about a minute before I was totally exhausted. The deer widened the gap between us without any signs of slowing down.

I finally gave up and coasted to a stop. I was bent over forward, resting my hands on my knees as I watched him disappear into the brush. He was gone. As I was trying to catch my breath, I noticed a sensation like warm water running down my leg. I looked down to see a sight that almost sent me into shock. I was wearing an old pair of Chuck Taylor All Stars at the time. I saw blood running through the laces of the high-tops. Standing straight up now, I looked at the inside of my right leg only to see more blood pulsing through a hole in my jeans. I had somehow accidentally stabbed myself while chasing the buck through the woods. There was so much blood I figured I had cut the artery on the inside of my thigh. I used the palm of my hand to put pressure on the wound and headed for the bridge. As I frantically hopped along, the bleeding seemed to get worse. I slowed down and walked the rest of the way out of the woods. When I arrived at the highway, Kristi was nowhere to be found. I walked over to the bridge and lay down beside it in order to prop my leg up on the guard railing. I lay there silently for about five minutes before I heard the beautiful sound of car tires approaching. Thank God it was her. I flagged her down and jumped inside the car. Kristi turned white as a sheet when she saw all the blood soaking through my pants. She tried to ask questions before I stopped her and said, "Don't talk...just drive." She rushed me to the emergency room in Commerce, Texas. Once I was lying on a gurney in a hospital, I relaxed a little.

"How many stitches will that take doc?"

The doctor advised me stitches would not be sufficient to close that stab wound. Four metal staples did the trick. I hadn't cut the artery after all and a week later I was good as new. Looking back on that day in the woods, it was two warriors that met, and both limped away wounded. I hope the old buck recovered enough to fight again another day. I knew better than to trail a wounded deer without a rifle, but it was a lesson I had to learn all over again.

SUREFIRE

SHOOTING DEER OFF THE ROAD used to be the preferred pastime for outlaws in Red River and Delta Counties. It seemed like every time I turned around I was getting a call from some landowner complaining about someone in a pickup truck shooting across his property from a road. Try as I might, it was hard to get a handle on the road hunting situation up there. When things got particularly bad in an area, I would break out "Surefire," my full-bodied buck deer decoy. *Surefire* was actually a generic term for several deer decoys made out of Styrofoam. He could be rigged with fancy electronics...or not. He was sometimes standing...or lying down in a resting position. Whatever the situation called for, I had a version of Surefire that would fit.

He was braver than most deer. Many times, I watched him stand his ground as bullets struck him time and time again. With each hit, he stood proud and erect, unwavering in his devotion to his cause. Surefire was a courageous Styrofoam soldier in the unending battle against poaching. You have to wonder what is going through a man's mind when he unloads four rounds of .270 ammo into a deer, then reloads and fires four more rounds, without any results. Surefire could bring out the worst in folks; he seemed to cast a spell on some. I've seen people crawl on hands and knees through briars and bramble just to get close enough to get a picture of him. After watching Surefire do his thing for many years, there is one thing I can say. You never know what people are going to do when they see a buck deer and they have a loaded rifle in the seat beside them.

Back in 1999, ole Surefire helped bring down one of the worst of the worst. There was a fellow operating in southern Hopkins County who was notorious for hunting deer from the road. He had a reputation for it and he liked it. He loved to brag about his exploits. Since Hopkins County was not my assignment, I didn't worry too much about what was going on down there. I had my hands full in my own county. However, I was aware that the two previous partners of mine struggled to catch the notorious road hunter that I will just call Buford.

Finally, a new warden was assigned to the county. Sean Reneau showed up and wasn't having any of it. Sean asked for my assistance and together we set out to put an end to Buford's evil ways. It really didn't take long. Late one afternoon around Thanksgiving, Sean and I picked a lonely blacktop road near the suspect's house, two miles away. Buford was no fool and had years of experience to guide his road hunting pursuits. So, I decided to employ the lying down version of Surefire. Few hunters were aware of this version. After carefully and strategically placing him in the center of a hay meadow, Sean and I hid behind a large stack of hay on the other side of the road.

Things were very slow at first. Not more than a couple of vehicles passed by in a one-hour period. They never even slowed down. Sean and I passed the time gossiping and swapping war stories. At 5:15 p.m., we could hear the sound of a vehicle turning off the highway onto the county road. It was dusky dark when the SUV slowly rolled by. It was him...Buford showed up. Sean turned on the video camera and we both held our breath. He spotted Surefire and slammed on the brakes. After a couple of tense seconds, he sped away.

Sean was pissed. "What the hell...why didn't he shoot?"

"Because he is going to turn around and come back with the deer on the driver's side." I had this all figured out.

Like clockwork, he did come back. He stopped right in front of us with our camera rolling. BOOM! He fired. BOOM! He fired again. Sean and I jumped the barbed wire fence and blocked the road ten yards in front of his vehicle. Buford pulled the rifle back inside the window and looked straight at us. The sight of two Texas State Game Wardens standing in the road with pistols drawn caused him to turn off the engine and raise his hands. It was over. His lifetime of poaching, left unchecked, just ended. Attaboy, Sean!

Chief Tallgrass

IT TOOK FORTY-SEVEN LONG YEARS of waiting but I finally got my Indian name.

Let me explain. It's my understanding of Indian tradition that a warrior was given his name by other members of his tribe after some meaningful event occurred in his life. Since Indian people were so closely tied to nature, a name many times ended up representing an animal, a weather event, or a physical feature on the land. Being the fierce wannabe warrior that I was, I long waited in vain for my Indian name to be bestowed upon me so I could take my rightful place in history alongside other great warriors. Warriors such as Crazy Horse, Sitting Bull, and Blue Duck. I finally got the name. Now let me tell you how it all happened.

Having taken a day off of work, my son, Erik, and I had spent most of the day deer hunting. Late in the afternoon, we left our deer stand disappointed at not seeing any deer. As we made the long walk back to the truck, a spike buck suddenly appeared in the trail one hundred yards in front of us. After a brief whispered discussion, Erik decided to take the buck. At the crack of the rifle, the deer went down. But to our surprise the deer got back to his feet, bounded into the chest-high grass, and disappeared. Erik and I walked to the spot where we had last seen the deer. There we found no blood trail, no tracks, no nothing. I could see the disappointment in Erik's young eyes. I said, "Don't worry son, we will find your deer."

We rushed home and grabbed a bite to eat. Then I called friend and master tracker Jake Needham to ask for help in finding the deer. As I was gathering up flashlights, Erik's mom reminded him of his homework. She put her foot down, so it looked like Erik wouldn't get to finish his hunt. Again I could see Erik's disappointment. Knowing he wouldn't get to concentrate on his studies anyway, I told him, "Come on son, you go with me, homework can wait." After getting Kristi's OK, we were off. We met Jake on the prairie west of Bogata and the search for the deer began. The three of us, using flashlights, searched back and forth across the field without any luck. After about forty-five minutes of searching, things were looking bleak. Our flashlights were getting dim and we were about to throw in the towel.

As we were making one last pass in the four-foot-tall grass, I veered to the south a little and almost stepped on the deer. I yelled to Jake and Erik and they came running. A big smile came across Erik's face once he laid eyes on his prize. Erik then looked up and asked, "Dad, how in the world did you ever find this deer in all this grass?"

Wanting to impress him with my savvy, I said, "Son, you just have to have the Indian ways."

Jake sniggered and said sarcastically, "I guess that makes you Chief Tallgrass."

BAM...just like that. It hit me like a ton of bricks when I realized Jake had just given me my Indian name. The circumstances didn't exactly fit Indian tradition but they were close enough for the girls I go with. Chief Tallgrass...yeah, I like that...has a ring to it. But two issues came up in my mind. First, "Am I a chief?" I reasoned that because I wear the pants in my family, I was the chief of my tribe. With that issue out of the way, I wondered if Chief Tallgrass was a good name at all. It could easily be confused with another, much less flattering name that rhymed with Tallgrass.

What the heck...I liked the name.

Barking In The Night

THE SUN HAD JUST GONE DOWN when my phone rang. The sheriff's department dispatcher was on the line. She advised me one of their deputies had just taken a call from a distraught woman who said her husband and five-year-old son had not returned home from an early morning duck hunt on Lake Tawakoni. The dispatcher went on to explain that deputies had located the missing man's truck and boat trailer at the Caddo Landing boat ramp. The truck was locked and the trailer was empty. There is certain information that an experienced game warden hears that instinctively causes him to know things are probably going to turn out really bad. What I had just been told caused me to have those uneasy thoughts.

I called my partner Gary Miller and asked him to meet me at the boat ramp with his patrol boat. I then gathered my gear, hugged my wife, and headed to the lake. Along the route to the lake, I tried to imagine what had happened to the missing father and son. A strong thunderstorm had swept across the lake early that morning just about the time duck hunters would have been launching boats. I wondered if weather might have played a role. My hope was that they may have just had boat motor problems and were simply stranded somewhere out on the lake. In that scenario, it would be as simple as locating them and towing them to shore. I was concerned that a five-year-old boy was involved. It was early January and the elements were not favorable for a kid that young to be out on the lake for an extended amount of time.

Gary and I arrived at the boat ramp about the same time and met with the deputy that took the original call. Everything was just as had been reported to me. Boat trailer was empty, truck was locked and secure. There were no clues that gave any indication of where the father-and-son hunters were at. The deputy stated that when he spoke to the wife over the phone, she had relayed to him that she had talked to her husband and son as they were leaving home before daylight that morning. She was told they would return sometime around midday. She never heard from them again.

Gary and I launched the patrol boat. I asked the deputy to stay in contact with the family member in case any more information became available. Lake Tawakoni is a very large lake by Texas standards...thirty-nine thousand acres. Much of the lake is open water; however, there are also large patches of water filled with stumps and old standing trees. Without any solid information to go on, Gary and I fell back on our personal duck hunting experiences on the lake. We simply asked ourselves, "If I left this boat ramp to duck hunt, where would I go?" We both agreed that a well-known island to the east that sat about one hundred yards off a peninsula was the answer.

When we left the ramp, there was not even a slight ripple across the water. The lake was dead calm. We used handheld spotlights to carefully search the shoreline as we cruised eastward. A bright full moon overhead helped us navigate around stumps and other wooden boat docks that extended out into the lake. After an hour of looking, we arrived at the big island. We circled it twice, looking for anything. After finding nothing, we anchored and killed the engine. We spent several minutes blowing a horn and yelling the names of the missing pair. No response at all. Just to make sure they were not on the island, I got out on foot and searched, with no results. We then continued to search the shoreline, looking for any signs.

It was about eleven o'clock when the weather changed. The moon became covered with clouds and a cold wind picked up out of the north, considerably, and continued to increase with each passing minute. Gary pointed the patrol boat toward the ramp and we searched all the way back. When we nosed the boat up against the shoreline at the ramp, the deputy came down to speak with us. I asked him, "Have you heard anything else?"

"No.... I just got back from a call about a stray dog acting weird on the other side of the lake."

"What do you mean, acting weird?"

"A lady reported a dog walking the shoreline, barking at the water."

"Did you see the dog?"

"Yeah, but he wouldn't let me get close to him."

"Give me the number of the lady who reported the dog."

Hmmmmm.... This was very interesting. I called the lady and identified myself as a game warden. I asked her when she had first seen the dog. She stated that he showed up just after daylight and had been walking the edge of the lake all day. I then asked her to describe the dog.

"It's one of those hunting type dogs."

"You mean a retriever?"

"Yeah, one of those kind.... He is still here.... He is barking right now."

At this point, Gary said, "Do you hear that? I can hear him."

Very faintly, over the wind and the waves, a dog could be heard barking across the large cove on the south shoreline. I asked the deputy to call the wife of the missing man and ask if he left the house that morning with a dog. A couple of minutes later, he came back with an answer…affirmative. It was very obvious now what was going on. That dog was trying to tell a story and no one was listening.

We cranked the motor, turned the boat around, and headed in a straight line toward the spot we last heard the animal. About three hundred yards later, we encountered a stump field. We had to slow to idle speed to maneuver through the timber. As I stood on the bow of the boat with a flashlight, I was trying to help direct Gary when I saw something to my right. It appeared to be a camo garment of some kind, draped over a stump slightly above the waterline. I motioned to Gary and he spotted it, too. When the nose of the boat was hovering over the object, I lowered myself down on both knees and reached down into the water to grab it. It was no object, it was a child.

After pulling the child's lifeless body into our boat, our hearts sank. We realized it was too late, there was nothing we could do. Gary quickly tied a marker buoy to a nearby piece of standing timber. We then returned to the ramp as quickly as we could safely get there. After first responders and other officials arrived, we turned the child over into their care and headed back out into the lake. It was close to midnight when we relocated the marker. The wind was stiff and waves constantly pushed us against stumps, hindering our search. After thirty more minutes, all we had for our efforts was a bag of decoys found floating in the timber. We conferred with our captain on the phone and decided to call off the search until first light in the morning. I didn't get much sleep that night. I kept replaying the terrible discovery I had made that night over and over in my head. Drownings are always terrible to work. When a child is involved, they are almost unbearable.

When the sun began rising over the lake the next morning, I was walking the south shoreline. A mile of walking produced only a cooler full of food and drinks from the stricken boat. At 8:00 a.m., Game Wardens Chris Fried, Grant Moore, and Dewayne Noble showed up with patrol boats. The four of us returned to the spot where Gary and I were the night before. It didn't take long to locate the missing boat about one hundred yards away. It was submerged, except for the nose of the boat. The weight of the motor was holding it vertical in the water. We were able to pull the short narrow flat-bottom out of the lake and place it across the bow of our much larger patrol boat and transported it to shore. An inspection of the boat offered no clues to what might have transpired the previous morning.

Returning to the marker buoy a third time, we began the unpleasant task of using handheld body drags in an attempt to locate a second drowning victim. Without anything to go on and stumps everywhere, it was going to be like finding a needle in a haystack. But we got lucky. Assuming the man and his son would have stayed together to the end, if possible, we began dragging around the area where the young boy had been found. Our hunch was correct. I found the father about twenty-five feet away. The recovery of the man's body put an end to the tragic episode. It was one of the saddest drownings I ever worked as a warden. The next week, a wooden cross was erected at the boat ramp. In the days and weeks that followed, it turned into a memorial adorned by duck calls, decoys, pictures, and other tokens left behind by loving family members and friends. The uniform name plates of the four game wardens that responded to the drowning were nailed to the cross as a token of support to a grieving family.

No Shirt, No Shoes, No Problem

I WAS LESS THAN ENTHUSIASTIC as I backed my patrol truck into the barn fifty yards off the highway. It was getting late in the hunting season and I had staked this spot out several times since October without any success. Still, it was a notorious stretch of roadway known far and wide to night hunting poachers. The narrow farm-to-market highway ran north and south and was lined with farm fields that attracted feeding wildlife, especially deer. In the distance, a second highway came east from Deport, Texas, and intersected my pavement just over the crest of a hill to my left. I leaned the seat back and got comfortable.

I listened to the AM radio station for over an hour. A handful of vehicles had passed by but none of the drivers even so much as tapped the brakes. Just before midnight, I had decided it was going to be another dry run. But then I observed a vehicle on the highway coming out of Deport. It was traveling a little slower than the speed limit and seemed to get progressively slower. All of a sudden, the headlights went out and the vehicle continued traveling east. I could clearly see the vehicle was still moving because the driver had his foot on the brake pedal. At this point I was waiting for a spotlight to light up the fields along the roadway. A spotlight was never used. I then guessed that maybe

42

these were hunters but they were using one of the new thermal units that were on the market. I rolled down my window to listen for any shots that might come. The vehicle kept slow rolling until it disappeared behind a hill in the distance. After a few seconds, I assumed the vehicle had arrived at the intersection of the two highways. Would he turn left and pass in front of me? Or would he turn right and drive over the horizon in the opposite direction? I hesitated for a few seconds, waiting to see if I could detect the glow of headlights approaching. When I didn't, that was it. I have never been accused of having any patience. I knew if he turned right and I didn't follow, I would lose him. There was a three-quarter moon that produced plenty of light to drive by. I started the engine and came out of my hiding spot blacked out. I crossed the ditch and hit the highway, headed south.

At the crest of the hill, I expected to see headlights in the distance going away from me. Confused, I sped up, trying to find the vehicle. Approaching the intersection, I found it. The vehicle was stopped in the roadway at the intersection with all lights turned off. I had no clue what was going on but I knew that, at the very least, I had a dangerous traffic violation. Plenty of cause to stop the vehicle and contact the driver. I turned off of Highway 410 and met the truck, front bumper to front bumper, in the intersection. When I flipped on my headlights and red and blue emergency lights, I could clearly see the driver talking on a cell phone. He had been totally unaware of my presence and became startled. He dropped the phone and started the truck's engine. Fearing he was about to flee, I exited my patrol truck and ordered him to turn the engine off. He complied. I then told him to show me his hands. He again complied. This cooperation gave me enough confidence to walk to the passenger-side window.

Through the open window, I identified myself as a game warden and asked the driver to explain what he was doing. He went into a long, drawn-out, incoherent tale that made no sense. His speech was slow and slurred. His eyes were bloodshot and droopy. Two pretty good indicators that he was drunk. When I asked to see the man's driver's license, he became verbally combative and demanded to know on what authority I could ask for his license. This is the point where things went south and I made a mistake that could have cost me dearly. I told the man to exit his vehicle. I then walked around the rear of the truck. The camper shell mounted on the truck caused me to lose sight of the man temporarily. He would have had plenty of time to retrieve a weapon. As I came around, I could see he had ignored my request to get out. Now, standing outside his window, I leaned in close enough to view the interior. What I saw made my heart skip two beats. There was a paddle-style pistol case unzipped and open, lying between his feet. Upon seeing this, I drew my pistol and held it close to my leg.

"Do you have a gun in that truck with you?"

"Yes, I do...right here."

"Mister, from this point on you better listen to what I tell you very closely and do not touch that gun...do you understand?"

"No, I don't understand why you are hassling me."

"Keep your hands where I can see them and get out of the truck."

"Why?"

I pulled open the driver's door and stepped back. Although he kept his hands on the steering wheel where I could see them, he refused to get out. Here again, my lack of any patience could have been a problem. After one more order to get out, with no results, I created the results I wanted. After holstering my pistol and dropping my flashlight to the ground, I lunged into the cab and grabbed the man around the neck and jerked him out of the truck. After taking him to the ground, I retrieved my flashlight and used it to inspect the inside of the cab. There, tucked between the seat and the center console, was a large automatic handgun.

I slammed the door shut as the man got back up on his feet. A scuffle now broke out. He was cursing and trying to get back inside the truck and I was trying to keep him out. I tried simply to push him backward away from the door. He was larger and stronger than I was, so that was a battle I was going to lose. I was fully aware that if he was able to get back into the truck, I would have to assume the worst for my own protection and shoot the man. That was something I didn't want to do.

I pulled the can of pepper spray from my duty belt and coated his face and neck. It only seemed to enrage him. He grabbed me, and what was a scuffle turned into a wrestling match that ended up in the ditch. Luckily for me, the man was intoxicated and I used that against him. His balance was poor and I was able to trip him off his feet twice. Both times he lost a shoe. However, I couldn't keep him down and he was fighting too wildly for me to put handcuffs on him. I ended up using his shirt to try and control him. His shirt was completely torn off in the process. As the struggle continued, I was finally able to get him face down and get one side of my handcuffs on one wrist. However, his shoulders were too broad and his wrists were too thick to apply the second cuff. It was going to take two sets of handcuffs and I didn't have time for that. I did the next best thing that I could think of at the time. I latched the second cuff to his belt loop behind his back. At least now he was partially subdued. This bought me some time.

I pushed him flat to the ground as I sprang to my feet and ran to his truck. After opening the door, I reached in and grabbed the handgun. I then ran to my truck and secured it.

Now the main threat had been removed and I was ready to put an end to this foolishness. I returned to the man to see if his attitude had changed. He was aware of what I had just done and it took all the fight out of him. Up on his knees in the muddy ditch, with one arm behind his back, he stretched out the other arm and said, "I'm done, I don't want to fight no more." I helped the man to his feet and escorted him to my truck where two sets of handcuffs were used to properly restrain him. An ambulance was summoned to the scene to decontaminate him from the effects of the pepper spray. Order was restored and he was transported to jail to face several charges. The least of which was driving while intoxicated.

The following afternoon, I received an unexpected phone call from the man's brother. I was defensive at first, anticipating I was about to get an ass chewing for doing my job. The call turned out to be quite informative and pleasant in the end. I was told the man I arrested was a really good person and had served his country in both Iraq and Afghanistan. I was also informed that after leaving the military and returning to civilian life, he had suffered from severe depression and had encountered many personal problems. His brother went on to explain that he was the person on the phone with him when I showed up. He said his brother had made statements that led him to believe that he was about to commit suicide. When I heard this, it all made sense. I do believe that I showed up just in time to prevent the man from taking his life. I think he fought so hard to get back in the truck so he could use his gun to finish a task he had decided on prior to my arrival. Anyway, the kind man on the phone thanked me for arresting his brother and then thanked me for my service. I, in turn, thanked him for his support. These types of phone calls were few and far between.

46

BAD WEATHER

BEING A GAME WARDEN requires that you work outside a lot. That's what I liked most about the job. However, if you're going to be outside all the time, there will be times that you are at the mercy of Mother Nature, be it good or bad. And brother, believe me when I say I've seen my fair share of really bad weather.

The terrible tornadoes in Canton, Garland, and Dekalb were just three of many disasters that I saw up close and personal. Looking back, of all the places I was stationed, Dalhart, Texas, had the most unpredictable weather. Unbelievable blizzards, dust storms, big tornadoes, and wildfires were common there.

Back on the other side of the state in East Texas, flooding was always the major weather-related problem. The one element of weather that got my attention faster than anything was lightning. One of the most frightening experiences I ever had occurred one afternoon when I parked at a locked gate and walked into a property to check a deer camp. It was about a quarter-mile trip through heavy timber. As I was walking in, a storm was approaching fast from the west. About the time I arrived at the camp and discovered it was empty, the first bolt of lightning struck an old oak only fifty yards from me. I turned around and began running toward my patrol truck. Another bolt slapped the ground right behind me. All that crap about lightning never striking twice in the same place is a fairy

47

tale. I had the truck in sight as I began to pray...literally. I made it out alive but I don't know how. Several bolts of lightning had struck all around me.

Of course, it wasn't always bad, and I enjoyed some really good weather while out on patrol. I kept a good tan in the summer months, that's for sure. Working outside late at night also gave me the opportunity to view some unusual cosmic events. Over the years, in addition to hundreds of brilliant falling stars, I witnessed two total lunar eclipses. For over two weeks in the spring of 1997, I gazed up in wonder every night at the Hale-Bopp comet as I patrolled the dam across Cooper Lake.

One night in Hartley County in the Texas Panhandle, I was sitting in a cornfield watching the horizon for approaching car lights. Suddenly, to the north, I saw the most beautiful sight. The aurora borealis, or the "northern lights," were lighting up the sky in a spectacular display of red and green curtain-like waves.

The unpredictable Texas weather made my career as a Texas Game Warden very interesting and memorable.

Recovery of a drowning victim. (Cooper Lake, Texas)

A spingtime tornado forms on the prairie as the warden keeps a safe distance. (Dalhart, Texas)

42 racoon hides hanging on a fenceline drying in the sun. Products of illegal trapping. (Birthright, Texas)

Illegal trapping in a state park almost cost this dog his life. (Cooper, Texas)

Over 100 crappie taken with nets. (Cooper Lake, Texas)

Flathead catfish taken by "electro-shocking" on the Sulphur River. (Kinsing, Texas)

Investigation of a large fish kill at a spillway. (Cooper Lake, Texas)

Removing a "hoop" net from the Sulphur River. (Naples, Texas)

Border patrol on the Rio Grande River. (Del Rio, Texas)

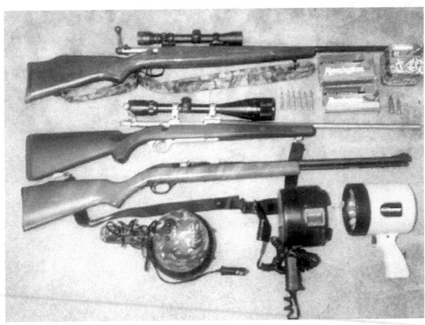

Equipment taken from road hunters at midnight. The rifles had all been reported stolen. (Dalhart, Texas)

You never know what you will find in the Texas desert. (Sierra Blanca, Texas)

Returning from air patrol with the Department of Public Safety. Wardens were often used as guides by agents looking for marijuana grow operations. (Paris, Texas)

Trailer loads of marijuana plants removed from
a public hunting area. (Dalby Springs, Texas)

Removal of a water pump hidden underground at a large
scale marijuana growing operation. (Delta County, Texas)

Game wardens observe as thousands of marijuana plants are burned then buried in a deep pit. (Delta County, Texas)

Questioning a suspect at the driver's door on a late night patrol. (Quinlan, Texas)

Sharpening the rifle skills at the firing range. (Pottsboro, Texas)

A hungry black bear prepares to enjoy lunch
under a corn feeder. (Clarksville, Texas)

A "rookie" warden completes alligator training at the academy. (Austin, Texas)

Standing next to a squad car at the end of a busy shift. Just days after a mass shooting took 5 officers' lives. (Dallas, Texas)

Warden Richards inspects a trophy antelope in the
Texas Panhandle (Dalhart, Texas)

A wooden cross was erected on the
shoreline as a memorial to a father
and son who drowned during a
duck hunt. It was adorned with
decoys, calls, pictures, flowers, and
the uniform name badges of the
wardens that responded to the call.
(Lake Tawakoni, Texas)

DALLAS

AFTER MANY YEARS of answering calls as a game warden, I learned to expect the unexpected. The very nature of warden work can, at times, keep a man off-balance. Half the time you are working out of a truck on dry land. The other half you are in a boat on some large body of water. The large variety of situations wardens get called to requires training, experience, and special equipment. A seasoned game warden knows all this and prepares accordingly.

July of 2016 was a stormy month in Texas and huge thunderstorms did a lot of damage and cost some human lives. One of those storms brought torrential rain to the city of Dallas. In the early morning hours of July 5, an officer with Southern Methodist University was caught in a freak urban flood as he sat in his car. A wall of water swept his vehicle into a drainage canal and then into a nearby creek. When the officer abandoned his vehicle and tried to reach safety, he was washed away. I got the call shortly after daylight. Captain Steve Stapleton called to advise me of the situation and directed me to drive to Dallas and assist other wardens in trying to locate the missing officer. On the way to Dallas, I set the radio to a local news station where I listened to survivors' accounts of the previous night's storm and got the latest info on the missing officer.

Upon my arrival, I was assigned to walk the banks of Turtle Creek. I spent the entire day walking the maze of storm drains and concrete canals that intersected the creek. Several helicopters from different agencies assisted by searching Turtle Creek all the way to where it emptied into the Trinity River several miles away. Despite an abundance of manpower, the day ended without the officer being located.

At 9:00 a.m. the next morning, the search resumed. At this point, hope of finding the officer alive had faded. Searchers realized we were trying to locate a body. The second day ended just like the first. That night the captain called me again. It was decided that wardens were going to try "dragging" Turtle Creek. I was told to bring my boat with me the next day.

The sky was clear and bright when the sun came up on July 7. Traffic was heavy as I weaved my way along Interstate 30, pulling the 16-foot flat-bottom boat on a trailer. At the top of the hour, the local news station briefly mentioned the ongoing search for the SMU officer. Most of the chatter on the radio was about a march and demonstration planned for downtown Dallas that afternoon. I arrived at the small park located on the bank of Turtle Creek, where I met Stormy McCuistion. Stormy had also brought his boat. After launching the two boats, our small team of wardens went to work doing a job we were all too familiar with…finding drowning victims. If experienced wardens have a precise location to drag, they are very efficient at locating a body on the bottom. However, without that precise location the task can be long and difficult. We spent the entire day in the aluminum boats in ninety-eight-degree heat. We were sunburned and exhausted when we were called off the water. We had spent three full days searching without any success and no one had any new ideas on how or where to look next.

We loaded the boats back on the trailers and all wardens fanned out in different directions, headed back to their counties. The forty-five-minute drive back home for me turned into an hour and a half because of the bumper-to-bumper traffic. Passing through Greenville, and starving, I stopped to grab a bite to eat. I finally walked into the back door of my home about eight o'clock. Kristi was already in bed watching TV when I came into the bedroom. After taking off my boots and gun belt, I lay across the bed and began to give her an update on my day and the search for the missing officer. I assumed my day was over. Not even close.

At nine o'clock, reporters on local news stations began to frantically report about a mass shooting in progress at the protest march in downtown Dallas. It was reported that at least two gunmen had opened fire on police officers and numerous officers were down. Upon hearing this disturbing news, I jumped off the bed and began putting all my equipment back on. Kristi asked, "Where are you going?"

"I'm going back to Dallas…. This is bad."

I told her I would keep her updated and then ran to my truck. After unhitching my boat trailer, I was on my way. On the interstate, I flipped on the red and blue lights, set the cruise control on ninety, and moved into the left lane. Local radio reports were giving horrific reports of between ten and twenty officers shot, some fatally. Twenty-five minutes later, as I crossed into Dallas County, my cell phone rang. It was Captain Steve Stapleton.

"Hey man, I don't know if you are aware of what's going on but I need you to get your stuff and go to Dallas."

"Captain, I'm already here."

"What do you mean?"

"I already heard about it and headed this way…. I'm ten minutes out."

"Ok good…. There will be a game warden supervisor and other wardens showing up soon. Find them and stay together."

"10-4 Captain."

Without radio communication with Dallas Police, or the sheriff's department there, I really had no idea about the exact location where I needed to be. I relied on local news radio reports that led me to the corner of Main Street and Lamar Street in downtown. Headed north, I encountered a DPD motorcycle lying on its side in the center of the intersection. The scene was still chaotic. Police were everywhere and streets were beginning to be closed. Bystanders were milling around taking selfies and adding to the confusion. However, there was a strange silence all around.

Staying in my patrol truck, I began to circle the area while watching other officers' actions in an attempt to determine where I was most needed. Several blocks away from downtown, I observed a convenience store that had been completely taken over by street thugs. There were twenty-five to thirty of them in the parking lot yelling and screaming profanities at police who were surrounding the building. There were another twenty-five to thirty inside the store. I was about to get out and assist the outnumbered officers when I saw two game warden trucks pass by. I fell in line and followed them to a park area at Commerce and Griffin Streets, where we parked. I got out armed with an M4 rifle, as did the other wardens. We went to work helping Dallas Police completely shut down the area and set up a large perimeter.

Over the next hour, fifteen Texas Game Wardens had arrived, along with many other officers from different agencies. It was still a tense time because of the lack of information. No one knew if there were armed suspects still at large. At about eleven o'clock, we got our first informal briefing. We were told two suspects had been arrested and another gunman had barricaded himself in a parking garage two blocks away. In addition, we were advised that the same gunman had threatened to detonate bombs that he had planted all around the downtown area.

A chain of command was formed, with an agent from the ATF taking the lead over the staging area where wardens and other officers had amassed. Calm was restored and nothing happened over the next two hours. Then, shortly before one o'clock, the agent in charge gathered all officers together and told us to get ready. He explained that negotiations with the gunman had broken down and police were going to use an explosive device to try and put an end to the situation. Not long afterward, we were told it was over. The suspected gunman was dead.

At this point we were all divided into small three-man teams. Three officers and a K-9 to each team. Game Warden Grant Moore and I, along with the dog and its handler, were assigned to search and clear a parking garage at the intersection of Commerce and Lamar Streets. We completed our assignment without any further incident. We remained in the area until told we were no longer needed.

The tragic event was over for me. I arrived back home shortly before daybreak. The next morning, the grim details of the previous night's massacre were fully revealed. After a large demonstration, eight hundred marchers and one hundred police officers were beginning to disperse when a lone gunman opened fire with a rifle. Twelve officers were shot. Five of the officers died of their wounds. At least two pedestrians were also wounded. It was the deadliest single incident for US law enforcement since September 11, 2001. The nightmare was crippling to Dallas Police. Many agencies pitched in to help an already understaffed force in the weeks that followed. Myself and numerous other game wardens spent the next week in

Dallas patrol cars, answering calls with their officers. We responded to shoplifting calls, family violence calls, stolen vehicles, burglaries in progress...all of it.

That week reminded me of my time as a street cop when I was with Richardson PD. That week also reminded me of the thankless job cops do every day in large cities. I was proud to say I responded that night in Dallas. I was also honored to ride along and assist DPD in their time of need. However, I was more than glad to get back to my county and the job I had as a Texas State Game Warden.

EUGENE

ASK ANY GAME WARDEN that has ever worked and he or she can quickly pick out one individual in their county who was simply a pain in the ass. The individual might not necessarily be a bad person, and could be an aggravation for different reasons. In my particular case, one name stands out above the rest...Eugene Dobbins.

Eugene had two problems. He was a spoiled-rotten only child from an influential family in the county. His uncle had a prominent position in county government, which meant he thought he could get away with anything. I first met Eugene very soon after arriving at my first assignment in Delta County. In fact, he was the first person I ever issued a written citation to. That citation was for shooting doves off of highline wires out of the window of his old pickup truck. Eugene had three pastimes that were near and dear to his heart. Hunting illegally, stealing anything that wasn't tied down, and drugs. All three of these undesirable habits put Eugene and me on a constant collision course.

Late one December night, I was headed to the North Sulphur river bottoms near the community of Lake Creek. I was pretty sure someone was shooting deer at night up there, and I wasn't having any of it on my watch. As I turned off of Highway 24 onto Farm Road 128, I noticed something different about an old tin-covered barn that sat fifty yards off the roadway. I had been past that barn hundreds of times and never once had I ever seen anyone around it. Driving slowly by the barn with my headlights turned off, I could see the door was slightly open and there was a light on inside. A closer look and I could see someone moving around inside. I wondered to myself, "What would someone be doing in that barn at one o'clock in the morning?" It was time to check it out.

I backed up beside the barn and quietly stepped out. Standing at the door, I peered inside. Well, guess who? It was Eugene Dobbins. Eugene was standing behind a Chevy truck along with his right-hand man at the time, Lotus Riggs. As I continued to watch with an ever-growing interest, Eugene and Lotus began trying to throw a rope over a rafter. This was more than I could stand. I knew what a rope hanging from a barn rafter probably meant, and I couldn't wait to see the deer. Looking back on it, I should have just sat tight and listened for a while, but I never did have much patience.

I gave the barn door a good shove and stepped inside. As sarcastically as I could, I asked, "Well, well, well, Eugene, what do we got here?" His eyes bugged out, his mouth fell open, and he just began mumbling incoherently. Lotus never missed a beat. He just kept tying the rope off as if I wasn't there. I eased up to the passenger-side door of their truck and had a look inside. Lying against the front seat were two high-powered scoped rifles. I also spied a Q-Beam spotlight and a couple of boxes of ammo. Continuing to the back of the truck, I looked over into the bed. There was a bunch of junk back there and a four-wheeler. At first I didn't see anything incriminating as Eugene began asking me, "What's up? What's up?"

Still snooping around the tailgate area of the truck, I asked Eugene, "What are y'all doing in here?" Before he could answer, I noticed wet blood dripping off the bumper. I took a closer look inside the bed of the truck and discovered a big buck was hidden underneath the four-wheeler. I had them now.

Eugene immediately went into his usual "why are you picking on me now" routine. He told me he had shot the deer earlier in the day, just before sundown, and was just now getting around to skinning it. He offered up a handful of more lies before I told him he was wasting his breath. The deer had blood dripping out of its nose, and it was as limber as a dishrag. At this point, I did exactly what I was trained to do at the academy, which, in the end, turned out to be a huge mistake. I retrieved a tape measure and a probe thermometer from my evidence kit that I carried in my truck. I took the dead animal's temperature, which measured ninety-nine degrees. I then measured the size of the deer's pupils and determined that they were still almost fully dilated. In my estimation, the big white-tail deer had been dead less than one hour. The only thing I wanted to know now was where it had been killed.

After some verbal sparring between the three of us, Eugene agreed to take me to the gut pile where he claimed the deer was taken. I confiscated the deer, all the guns and ammo, along with the Q-Beam, and followed Eugene and Lotus to a ranch five miles away. Once there, I inspected the guts, which were still very warm. Eugene became defiant and pointed in the direction of a deer stand about two hundred yards away.

"I was in that deer stand when I shot the deer."

"Oh, really.... Wait here, Eugene."

I walked through the muddy field to the stand. The stand was a very old wooden tower blind. I closely inspected the wooden rungs on the ladder that led up into the stand. There was no mud, dirt, or any moisture at all evident on them. Inside the stand sat an old wooden chair, complete with cobwebs. No one had sat in that chair in a very long time. I had seen enough. I knew a liar when I met one.

I allowed Eugene and Lotus to leave the scene. However, the next morning I got an arrest warrant for Eugene. I didn't have enough evidence to charge Lotus with anything that would stick. All of Eugene's backup within the county went right to work trying to get my case against him dismissed. Instead of calling me and discussing the case, along with the evidence I had collected, the local county attorney called my department in Austin and asked to speak to TPWD's forensic expert. The department never had such a thing. However, unbelievably, that same county attorney advised me later that he had been directed to a very "knowledgeable" warden. What a joke. That warden turned out to be a very egotistical officer who had worked a very long time in South Texas. Supposedly, he told the county attorney that I had made some mistakes while gathering physical evidence, and based on that he could not pursue the case. I decided right then I would never stick a thermometer up any deer's ass again. From that day forward, I used my common sense to determine when a deer was killed. I put it all in a report and turned it in. If there were any questions, I would explain it to a jury, face-to-face.

Sure enough, the county attorney asked the county judge to dismiss the case. However, to his credit, Judge Whitney was a good, honest man. Judge Whitney called me up to his office and explained the situation to me. Facing all local political heat, the judge told me, "This case might not ever get prosecuted, but I have the final say on whether it gets dismissed or not.... I may need to review it." He pitched the report up on his desk. For the next three years, the case folder sat on his desk, literally. He always pointed it out whenever I visited his office. He would wink and say, "It ain't going away."

Eventfully, I requested a transfer to Dalhart, out in the Texas Panhandle. One of the last things I did before I left Cooper was to go by Judge Whitney's office and put the matter to rest. The only consolation I was left with was that Eugene and Lotus didn't get to keep their prize buck. I took it from them the night it was killed and they never saw it again.

NIGHT HUNTERS

EVERY TEXAS GAME WARDEN gets the same excellent training at the academy. However, after leaving the training center, most wardens develop an area of expertise. They develop those special skills from working in an area of the state where a certain type of game warden work is required. For example, a warden working on the gulf coast might be very good at catching illegal shrimpers. There are wardens on the border with Mexico who are skilled at finding nets and sniffing out drug shipments coming across the Rio Grande. Other guys that worked the lakes a lot specialized in filing boating-while-intoxicated cases. The area of game warden work that felt like I was really good at and enjoyed above everything else was chasing night hunters. Northeast Texas, where I spent most of my career, was deer country, and we had no shortage of beer drinking rednecks. Throw in a rifle and a Q-Beam spotlight into the equation and a warden had his hands full. To be effective catching poachers shooting deer late at night, you need to be a night owl by nature and have some patience. You'll also need to know every muddy backroad in your county like the back of your hand since you spend a lot of time driving them late at night with no lights on.

When I first came on board in 1996, shooting a buck deer out of the window of a pickup truck after midnight was much more common. In the early days of my career, it wasn't hard

71

for me to nab two or three bunches on a good Saturday night. That all changed a few years later when the penalties for such behavior jumped up to the felony level. However, regardless of the threat of jail time, fines, restitution, or the possibility of losing your favorite rifle, there was always some knuckleheads willing to chance it. After years of dealing with the nighttime bandits, I got good at anticipating their next move. I didn't even come close to catching them all, but I caught enough to keep them on their toes and twisting their necks to look over their shoulder. It wasn't always a matter of skill. Sometimes it was just pure dumb luck and being at the right place at the right time.

Late one winter night in Red River County, I had a group stopped on a county road that intersected with Highway 410. They had a few minor violations that we were discussing. While standing outside the truck with the hunters, I could hear the sound of mud tires whining down the highway a half mile to the north. I looked up just in time to see the vehicle's brake lights come on as it abruptly came to a stop in the highway. After stopping, all the lights on the vehicle suddenly were turned off. This was of great interest to me because the exact spot where the truck stopped was a well-known spot deer frequently bedded down near the road. Now, I had a decision to make. I could deal with the violators in hand or go for a possibly bigger fish. I decided on the latter. I gave the men verbal warnings for the infractions then asked them to give me five minutes before turning on any lights and leaving. They were aware of what was going on and agreed. I quickly got in the patrol truck and drove off into the darkness.

Blacked out, I drove to the intersection of the dirt county road and the highway. There I watched and waited. I didn't have to wait long. Looking north out my side window, I saw all the lights come back on. The vehicle headed my way and it was in a hurry. As it passed by the front of my patrol truck, I turned on my headlights and fell in behind it. The driver maintained his speed at sixty miles per hour but he was all over the road from shoulder to shoulder. I had seen enough. I lit him up and pulled the truck over. Inside the truck, I found four heavily intoxicated men that included the driver. In the back, I found a large white-tail buck. An investigation revealed the buck had been shot an hour earlier. The unlucky poachers came back to retrieve their trophy unaware that conditions had changed and I was out lurking around. All four men were arrested on various charges. The truck was impounded. The rifle used to kill the deer was confiscated. The buck deer was seized as evidence. Just another night at the office.

Hog Wild

WHEN THE CLOCK STRUCK TWELVE with no luck to show for my patience, I decided to make a move. It was mid-January and I was trying to catch a night hunter using a spotlight to kill a deer. I had been sitting in a hiding spot watching a hay meadow that sat next to FM Highway 410 in far north Red River County. The area was notorious for illegal hunting from the roadway.

I left the cover of the trees and pulled out onto the pavement. I headed west. Slow rolling down the highway "blacked out," I searched the horizon for that familiar glow of a Q-Beam that every experienced warden who has ever worked could spot in an instant. This stretch of lonely highway was very secluded with very few homes. Any vehicles moving at this time of night in this area would attract attention. I had put four miles behind me when I rounded the big curve at a place known locally as Wright's Plantation. I was now headed south. At that very instant something caught my eye. There it was...what I had been looking for.

Across the open farm fields to my left, I observed the glow of a spotlight bouncing up and down on the horizon. I instantly determined the location where the light was being used. County Road 2356, a mile to the west, ran parallel to Highway 410. I stopped long enough to observe the light in order to figure out which direction it was headed. It was headed south and this was good news. It meant the hunters working the light would arrive in Kiomatia just ahead of me in about five minutes. All I had to do was beat them to that intersection and I would have them caught. Without concern of being detected, I reached down, flipped on my headlights, and punched it. Taking one last glance over my left shoulder, I could still see the spotlight. Looking back at the road in front of me... "HOLY CRAP, HOGS!"

I reached for the brake pedal but it was too late. BAM! I hit them. Lots of them. A long line of wild feral hogs that stretched from one ditch across the highway into the opposite ditch were crossing in front of me. There were twenty-five to thirty of them. I plowed through the herd at sixty miles per hour. The impact caused my truck to pull hard to the right and ended up stopped on the side of the road. When I got out, there were hogs squealing in every direction. Three big sows were lying dead in the highway. Two more big pigs made it as far as the fence line before giving up the ghost. Who knows how many limped off, severely injured.

After pulling the fresh bacon out of the roadway, I returned to my truck to do a damage assessment. There was plenty of damage to assess. The brush guard soaked up most of the damage. The top two brackets broke off, causing the brush guard to fold up under the front bumper. The wraparound sides of the guard were now pointing straight upwards. The front bumper was pushed backward into the side panels and also had slightly damaged the radiator. The front tires would still turn. However, I found out on the way home that at every sharp curve in the road, they would rub badly, shaving off rubber and ruining a new set of tires. Obviously, my night patrol came to a screeching halt...literally.

The spotlighters were now the last thing on my mind. I limped home in the damaged patrol truck. In Texas, drivers in rural areas have been dodging wild hogs for years. I had my own close calls with hogs and deer but had always been lucky. My luck finally ran out.

I'm Not Chasing
You Anymore

ONE DAY IN 2003 during the middle of deer season, I was headed to Ladonia, Texas, in Fannin County to meet game wardens Dale Waters and Eddie Hines for lunch. Eddie and Dale had been working the deer decoy on the Caddo National Grasslands that morning. "Bucky" had gotten shot a couple of times by road hunters and I wanted to hear all the details.

As I came out of the small community of Ben Franklin, westbound on Highway 128, I looked in the rearview mirror and noticed a vehicle approaching me from behind at a very high rate of speed. I thought to myself, "What the hell is the big hurry?" as the Lincoln Town Car passed me at about eighty miles per hour in a no-passing zone at the crest of a hill. At that point in my career, I had too much municipal police officer still in me and just couldn't resist the opportunity to pull the car over and give the driver a citation and probably a good chewing.

I hit the gas pedal and flipped on the red and blues. As I closed in on the back of the Town Car, I could see it was occupied by two men. The driver was closely checking me out in his rearview mirror. It appeared the passenger was busy hiding something underneath the front seat. I followed them for a couple miles before the driver finally pulled over to the side of the road and stopped with his car sitting half on the pavement and half on the grass. I had seen enough to know that someone was probably going to jail.

As I slowly got out of my patrol truck, I noticed both of the men in the car were turned and looking at me through the back windshield. The brake lights were illuminated, which told me the driver had his foot on the brake pedal, which probably meant the car was in gear. That little voice in my head was telling me, "This guy is going to run." Sure enough, as I was about halfway between my front bumper and his rear bumper, the driver slammed on the accelerator. I'm sure he thought he was going to get a good head start on me, but unfortunately for him, his rear wheel in the wet grass just started spinning. I ran back to my truck, jumped in the driver's seat, and shifted into drive as wet grass and soft mud was hitting my windshield. The big Lincoln finally spun its way onto the roadway and one hell of a vehicle chase was on.

The narrow two-lane highway between Ben Franklin and Ladonia was fifteen miles of hills and sharp curves. As I chased the bad guys at speeds between seventy and one hundred miles per hour, it was clear they had the better, faster vehicle. But I had two things the driver of the getaway didn't have...experience and training. Several times they would get a big lead on me only to run off the roadway at a curve, which would allow me to get right back in the chase. During the chase, two oncoming vehicles had to hit the ditch to avoid a head-on collision with the runners. One of those vehicles was an old farm truck pulling a round bale of hay on a trailer.

I closed the gap between me and them at the Delta County and Fannin County line. At this point, the passenger started throwing objects out his window. I had no doubt what he was throwing...illegal drugs. The chase continued into the city limits of Ladonia. The Town Car couldn't shake me as the driver raced up city streets, barely missing kids on bicycles and neighborhood dogs. I'm sure the two men in the car were now asking themselves, "Who is this guy?" I guess they finally gave up and switched to plan B: ditch the car and flee on foot. That's where they really made a big miscalculation. A foot chase against me absolutely guaranteed at least one of them was going to get caught.

With the vehicle still in motion, the driver opened his door and held it open with his foot. The passenger did likewise. As the car slowed, the dynamic duo of dumbasses bailed out in two directions as their ride continued rolling down the street. I was on the radio with the county yelling directions and asking for help as I slid to a stop and bailed out, running. As I began to chase the driver, I looked back over my shoulder and saw the passenger returning to the vehicle, which had now rolled to a stop in the ditch. The driver ran across an open field and then up an abandoned railroad right-of-way with me right behind him. As we ran along the tracks, he passed a man and woman on horseback. I yelled to the man on the horse to "Follow that guy!" He just looked at me like I was crazy and started pulling back on the reins as we went by. A lot of help they were.

The fellow I was chasing was about twenty years younger than me and pretty fast. I started thinking that he might get away. Suddenly, he took a hard left, ran across the street, and jumped a chain-link fence into a backyard. He then began running through backyards and jumping fences of the homes lined up along that street. We jumped a half dozen fences before he came to the last one. I was totally exhausted and knew if I didn't get him stopped pretty soon he was going to get away and all this chasing would have amounted to nothing. As he approached the last fence, I shouted, "I'm tired!" (huff, huff) "I'm not chasing you anymore!" (huff, huff) "Stop or I'll shoot you!"

He sailed over the fence but when his feet landed, he lay facedown on the ground. With four strides and a leap, I was on top of him. As I was handcuffing him, I could hear vehicles racing my way. I looked up to see the A-team was coming to my rescue. Two big green game warden trucks driven by Eddie and Dale. When the dust settled, Jernell Ike Green was under arrest for felony evading in a vehicle and an outstanding Fannin County warrant. The passenger was never positively identified.

At the Fannin County Sheriff's Office, I was busy completing a book-in sheet when I got a call from the Delta County dispatcher. She told me a citizen in Pecan Gap had witnessed the chase and picked up some of the items that had been thrown from Green's vehicle. I returned to Delta County and retrieved the items...a Buck knife and two small bags of white powder. At the Delta Count Sheriff's Office, Deputy David Short tested the powder. It tested positive for cocaine.

As a side note to this story, eight years later I was subpoenaed to testify at the punishment phase of a trial involving Green. He was arrested for selling an undercover cop some crack cocaine. He was sentenced to ten years in the Texas Department of Corrections.

TRAGEDY AT TIRA

AT 8:00 A.M., Warden Sean Reneau and I were flying down Interstate 30 in Hopkins County headed to a district meeting at the district office. My cellphone rang and on the other end was state park officer Glen Stone. Glen said, "Hey, Benny, I think we may have problem over here at the Tira boat ramp." The Tira boat ramp was a public boat ramp at the southeast corner of Cooper Lake dam. As a state park officer, part of Glen's duties included checking the ramp each morning. Glen told me he had found a car sitting in the parking lot there with the driver's-side door standing open, the engine running, and no one around. Glen also said he found a three-page letter lying in the front seat that sounded a lot like a suicide note. He didn't have to say any more, as I knew instantly that we did, indeed, have a problem.

Sean and I drove back to the ramp where we met Glen and a Hopkins County deputy that had also arrived. Upon our arrival, Glen had another bit of information. He advised us that just after calling me, the small car had run out of gas. Apparently, the car had been running for some time. I walked down to the edge of the lake where the boats launched. There, I found a blue jacket floating in six inches of water. Hmmmmm...this didn't look good. After retrieving the jacket and walking back up to the top of the ramp, I asked Glen to let

81

me have a look at the letter he had found. I read the letter, which never mentioned suicide or anyone about to harm themself. The letter did, however, leave me with the impression that the author was deeply depressed and in despair.

Sean and I decided to bring our boat to the ramp, as it was looking more and more like we were about to go into body-recovery mode. By the time we launched our boat into the lake, sheriff's investigators and first responders had arrived. Seated at the front of the boat, Sean looked back at me and asked, "Well, where do you want to start dragging?" Dragging referred to the use of a tool that wardens use to retrieve drowning victims off the bottom of a lake. It was a metal frame that had six short links of chain welded down the center. At the end of each chain was a very large treble hook.

I was just as in the dark about where to begin as Sean was. I tried to imagine what I would do if I was about to kill myself by jumping in the lake. I decided if I was going to do it, I would jump off the end of the wooden pier and start swimming away until I sank. It was mid-December so anyone swimming away from the pier, in the frigid water, wouldn't make it very far. About twenty yards from the end of the wooden pier, I lowered the drag into the water. It no more hit bottom before I felt something tugging on the rope. I figured I had snagged a log or something. Surely there was no way we had found him that quickly. I very slowly began to pull the rope back into the bottom of the boat. I was carefully pulling as, suddenly, a man's body emerged through the murky water. We had found our victim.

A later investigation by the sheriff's office revealed the young man drove to the boat ramp just after sunrise and took his own life. He was apparently upset over issues at school and a personal relationship that he was involved in. The really sad part was the fact that this young man seemed to have a lot to look forward to in life. He was an honor student at Texas A&M University in Commerce, Texas.

As a game warden, retrieving drowning victims was the part of my job that I dreaded the most.

TRICK OR TREAT

ON HALLOWEEN NIGHT IN 1997, I took my wife and our children to the local Halloween carnival at the school. Afterwards, we let Kaitlin do some door-to-door trick-or-treating on the way home. After we got back to the house, I told Kristi I was going to go out and work awhile. Back in those days I just couldn't get enough game warden work and rarely did I ever take a full day off. I put on my uniform, slipped into my gun belt, and headed out to catch a night hunter.

My plan was to go to a notorious night hunting area known as the Oyler Loop. There I would find a hiding spot and wait. However, I didn't get far out of the city limits of Cooper before I ran into trouble. I was headed south on Highway 24 about two miles out of town when I passed a man in the ditch walking back toward Cooper. My first thought was he probably had car trouble down the road somewhere. I decided to turn around and see if I could help him in any way. I spun the steering wheel, did a U-turn in the highway, and headed back. I grabbed the microphone and tried to check out with the county dispatcher. I got no response. My relationship with the sheriff's office at that time wasn't very good. If the truth was known, I think the sheriff, who disliked game wardens, probably instructed his dispatchers to screw with us by not answering us on the radio, me in particular.

As I pulled up on the shoulder of the highway behind the man, I tried the radio again. I still got no response. At this point the man, dressed in a long black "slicker coat," spun around and walked out of the ditch onto the highway. Something about the man's stride concerned me. I was a very safety-conscious officer with a good sixth sense about things. This man was sending out some bad vibes.

I flipped on my red and blue emergency lights and stepped out behind my open door. I could now clearly hear the man cursing as he got nearer to my truck. After one last unsuccessful attempt to give the county my location, I pitched the microphone into the front seat and stepped out and around my door to confront the angry man. As he got to the front of my truck, he suddenly bladed his body toward me, stepped behind my grill guard, and ran his right hand inside the long coat he was wearing. Instinctively, I drew my pistol and leveled off at his head. "Don't you move one more damn muscle!" I yelled at him. "Whatever's under that coat better stay there or I'll shoot your ass!" The man obviously took me seriously. He stood motionless like a statue with his right hand still concealed beneath his coat.

I moved around behind him and grabbed my shoulder microphone. "8214 county...I need help on 24 south now!" Immediately the dispatcher answered and dispatched two deputies. In the two minutes it took for the deputies to arrive, the angry and very intoxicated man began taunting me and at one point said, "You ain't man enough to shoot me." I assured him that if he pulled a gun out from under his coat, that would be the last thing he would do on this earth.

When the two deputies arrived, I told them I felt like the man had a gun underneath his coat. We surrounded the man and one of the deputies told him to slowly raise his hands over his head and lock his fingers. I then grabbed the right side of his coat and pulled it back, which revealed a 9 mm semiautomatic pistol stuck in the waistband of his pants. I removed the pistol and inspected it. It had a round in the chamber and ten more rounds in the magazine.

The deputies were familiar with the man and told me he hadn't been out of jail too long. Now, he was going right back. A further investigation into the man's activities that night uncovered the fact that he and his wife had a big argument over his drinking habits. She had kicked him out of the house thirty minutes prior to my arrival. That's how he ended up walking from Klondike to Cooper looking for a place to spend the night. The deputies escorted him to a nice comfortable bed at the county jail.

Do I think the guy would have shot me? He was drunk, angry, and he didn't like the police. Yes...if I had not drawn my pistol so quickly and convinced him that I would use it, I think he would have shot me. As a student of history, I had read many stories of lawmen in the old west. One of those lawmen in particular, Wyatt Earp, seemed to have the right approach. In dealing with bad men, he was direct, decisive, and had no hesitation. Wyatt Earp survived some dangerous encounters and went on to live a long and healthy life. I learned from those history lessons.

RIDE ALONG

IT USED TO BE THAT WARDENS could allow folks to ride along on patrol. It might be a close friend or family member that wanted to see firsthand what wardens do on a daily basis. Both my son and my father logged many miles sitting next to me. Many young men and women who aspired to become game wardens themselves also frequently asked to ride along. They wished to gain some actual experience and make a connection with a warden who could answer their questions about the career choice. Such was the case with young Colby Horn. Colby was a senior at the local high school. I met him through my daughter, who was also a student there. Even before meeting him, I knew enough about Colby to know he was a pretty good kid. He hunted and fished and was country as hell. So, I didn't have any reservations when he came to me and asked if he could go out on patrol with me.

I told him to be at my home in Johntown at dark. Colby showed up right on time and Kristi fed us before we struck out. There had been a lot of rain in recent weeks and water was being released out of Cooper Lake Dam. This always attracted local fishermen so I figured that would be a good place to start our night. We left my driveway and made the short drive to Highway 271. As I was turning south, Colby was chattering about his plans to one day become a game warden. I was all ears for about a mile and then it happened. I suddenly saw a man walking down the center of the highway. I jerked the steering wheel to the right and passed by the guy on the shoulder. He was wearing black jeans and was shirtless. I made a U-turn and came back to find the guy still walking down the center of the highway. I parked on the shoulder and flipped on my red and blue lights. While I was checking out with my county dispatcher, Colby asked, "What is he doing?"

"I don't know but he is going to get run over if I don't get him out of the road. Colby, stay in the truck and don't get out...understand?"

Colby nodded yes in agreement. Luckily, there was no vehicle traffic at the time, which was unusual. I approached the guy, who was now thirty feet away. Standing on the shoulder of the road, I yelled at him and motioned to come to me. He just threw up his left arm and began muttering something in Spanish while still cruising down the pavement near the center stripe. He was totally ignoring my commands. At this point, I could see the faint glow of headlights approaching from the north. It was time to remove him from the road.

I had observed him long enough to come to the conclusion that he was either very drunk or high on something. Carrying my flashlight, I quickly walked to the center stripe, grabbed the guy's left wrist, and began walking backwards, pulling him along to the side of the road. He began to protest immediately. He had been carrying a shirt in his right hand. He tossed it away in a fashion that caught my attention. Using the flashlight, I began to watch him carefully as I pulled him into the ditch. I noticed him put his hand behind his back. I attempted to spin him around but he kept turning away from me. Now, that little voice in my head was screaming at me...DANGER!

I spun him one more time, just in time to see him pulling a fixed-blade knife out of his back pants pocket. Still grasping his left wrist, I dropped my flashlight and reached up with my right hand to grab a handful of hair. With all the strength in my body, I jerked him backwards off his feet. He landed with a thud as I pulled my pistol from its holster. I didn't speak any Spanish but the language I was speaking was colorful and he seemed to understand every syllable of it. He laid his head back on the ground and stretched both arms out. He was lying on the knife. My hunch was correct. The guy was drunk…very drunk. His intoxication was actually a blessing. If he had been sober, he might have been coordinated enough to stab me. If he had been sober, I might not have been able to jerk him off his feet so easily. But then again, if he had been sober, this whole episode might not have ever happened.

Anyway, I was able to handcuff him and transport him to jail. Later that night as Colby and I talked about what had happened, I told him, "You remember what you saw tonight and remember how quickly things can go wrong. You can never be too careful." That nighttime patrol ended without any more troubles. Several weeks later, the man that I had arrested that April night was given time served in jail for his crimes and deported back to Mexico.

PARTNERS

BACK IN OUR YOUNGER DAYS, game warden Rick Lane and I were hell on wheels when it came to catching outlaws late at night. Whenever he would come up from Marion County to work with me, it was almost a guarantee that someone was going to jail. The two of us logged hundreds of miles and many late nights in pursuit of bad guys.

One late night out on patrol, Rick surprised me by asking, out of the blue, "Benny, you know why I like working with you?"

I answered, "No, why?"

"Because I feel safe.... I know that no matter what happens, I'm going home."

I was really honored by what Rick had said, especially since he had many more years' experience than me, and had worked with some damn good wardens before me. I felt the same way about Rick. No matter what kind of crap we found ourselves in, I knew he had my back. Little did we know at the time that confidence we had in each other would keep both of us safe more than once.

Rick called me up late one night and said he was on the way to my house. I knew that meant I would be out all night long and would watch the sun coming up the next morning. When he arrived, we got into my patrol truck and headed out on our latest law enforcement mission. After two or three hours of patrolling around Cooper, Enloe, and Pecan Gap, we had a few feathers in our cap. We had managed to locate and stop a couple of groups of night hunters and written citations for minor violations.

Just after 2:00 a.m., we decided to break some new ground so we slipped over the county line into Hunt County. As we did, we encountered a flatbed farm truck with someone inside shining a spotlight at the crest of a hill. As soon as the occupants of the truck spotted us, the spotlight was turned off.

"Dammit, Rick, they see us.... When we pass 'em, they'll know who we are."

Rick came back saying, "No, they won't.... Hit them with your bright lights just before you pass them."

It worked like a charm. I blinded them with my brights just as I passed by at fifty miles per hour. When we went over the hill, I turned off all my lights, hit the ditch, and did a U-turn. When we reversed course and came back over the hill, the flatbed truck was a half mile ahead of us, working the spotlight in the ditches again. Completely blacked out, I closed in and followed the flatbed truck back into Delta County. The driver of the truck continued to shine the ditches and the fields along the highway before turning south onto a muddy county road.

Rick and I had seen enough, so I rushed up behind the truck and turned on my red and blue lights. Surprisingly, we discovered there were two Hispanic men on the flatbed of the truck. One was holding a pump shotgun, the other was armed with an SKS semiautomatic rifle. Seeing the flashing lights, the driver brought the truck to an abrupt stop in the middle of the muddy road. The two men standing on the flatbed both laid down their guns and put their hands in the air without having to be told.

Unconcerned, Rick got out on his side and made his way to the front of my truck. We had seen this kind of thing a hundred times before. I stepped out and while standing beside the truck, I called the county on the radio to give the dispatcher our location. As I began to speak into the microphone, I saw the driver's side door of the suspect truck open and a fellow stepped out. At this point, it seemed like things were going in slow motion. That fellow took one look at Rick approaching and began to turn around. I clearly saw a pistol in his right hand. He turned his back to Rick and shoved the pistol down the front of his pants. I threw the microphone back inside the truck and yelled at Rick, "Gun...gun...he's got a gun!" I ran around my door as I pulled my pistol and kneeled down by my front bumper, ready to shoot if I had to.

The man seemed shocked to hear me yelling. I think he thought Rick was by himself. Rick drew his pistol and ordered him to throw up his hands. I kept a close eye on the other two men, who had laid down on the flatbed truck. The three men didn't speak much English but after staring down the muzzles of our pistols, they got the message. Rick holstered his Glock with one hand as he grabbed the driver in a choke hold with the other hand. He spun him around like a top and reached down the man's pants and came out with a 9 mm Beretta, fully loaded and ready to go.

With what limited Spanish I was able to speak, I ordered the two other men off the truck and handcuffed them. We found a video camera in the front seat of their truck. A review of the video inside showed the men shooting several rabbits off the roadway. At one point, one of the men went to retrieve a rabbit in a field. The video showed he came back to the truck, swinging the rabbit over his head in one hand while holding a bottle of Jack Daniel's in the other. The three men were newly arrived Mexicans. All three were in the country illegally, all three were drunk. None of the three had a driver's license or a hunting license. Most importantly, one of the three may have had murder on his mind.

In the end, I made sure Rick was safe and no matter what happened, he was going home. And no matter what other crap happened that night, or any other night, Rick had my back. Three Mexicans got to visit the Delta County jail.

VEHICLE CHASES

OF ALL THE DANGERS that law enforcement officers face in their careers, vehicle pursuits rate right up near the top as the most dangerous. A lot of things can go wrong during a pursuit, any one of which can get you killed in a hurry. Game wardens in particular face an even greater challenge due to the fact that they drive high-profile, four-wheel-drive trucks. A four-wheel-drive truck with mud tires was never intended to fly down the highway at over one hundred miles per hour and take sharp curves. Yet, that's the situation that more than one warden has found himself in.

Over the years, Texas Game Wardens have been involved in many chases and no two were ever exactly alike. A likely scenario for a vehicle pursuit involving a game warden might go like this. The warden tries to stop a vehicle in a pasture at midnight for shining a spotlight at a small herd of deer. The vehicle flees and the race is on to see who gets to the front gate first. If the warden blocks the gate, everything might be over right then and there. If the bad guys get through the gate, the chase usually proceeds down some dusty back road. One of four things might happen now. The bad guys might come to their senses and stop. On the other hand, they might also outrun the warden. The fleeing truck could flip on a curve and smash into a tree. But then again, so could the warden.

The stakes were raised for runners when the laws changed and fleeing in a vehicle went from being a misdemeanor to a felony. I was personally involved in numerous chases, both as a police officer and as a game warden. The most unusual vehicle chase I was ever involved in found me chasing a vehicle in reverse. That situation occurred very late one night as I was returning to my home near Rosalie, Texas, from night patrol. I lived on a lonely gravel road with only one neighbor. As I got within three hundred yards of my driveway, I encountered a vehicle coming toward me. It turned out to be a small Chevrolet S-10 Blazer. I knew for a fact that the driver was not one of my family members, nor did it belong to my neighbor. Obviously, I was curious as to who was prowling around my neighborhood at 2:00 a.m. I decided to find out.

I stopped in the roadway and turned on my red and blue emergency lights in an attempt to stop the vehicle. My intentions were for the vehicle to stop in front of my patrol truck. Instead, the small SUV accelerated, drove around me in the ditch, and hauled ass. As the vehicle went by, I got a good look at the scraggly white male driver. Rather than try to turn my vehicle around in the narrow roadway, I simply shifted into reverse and gave chase. I was gripping the steering wheel with my left hand and looking over my right shoulder out the back windshield. If the guy driving would have concentrated on his driving, he probably could have run off and left me. However, he was too busy grabbing objects out of the floorboards and throwing them out the driver's side window.... Drugs, I assumed.

I stayed close enough as the chase proceeded south on County Road 1305. When we reached the intersection at Highway 909, the driver pulled a stunt that Bo and Luke Duke might have tried. Taking a big risk without regards to oncoming traffic, he accelerated and jumped the highway to the other side and resumed the chase and continued to flee down the county road. At the intersection of 909, I did some fancy driving of my own, spinning my truck around in the center of the highway. Now I had my truck headed forward in the right direction.

I pinned the gas pedal against the floor and within a few seconds, I was on his back bumper. I guess the driver decided he wasn't going to be able to beat me, so he bailed out. Leaving his vehicle rolling down the center of the road, he ran to a large metal gate, shirtless and shoeless. He sailed over the gate and disappeared into the chest-high weeds. I calmly pulled up to the gate and exited my vehicle. It was mid-August so it was very hot and humid. I knew this guy wasn't going to go far. I climbed to the top of the gate and shined my flashlight out across the field. I knew full well that he was out there lying flat on the ground somewhere.

At this point, I had no intention of wading through that tall grass looking for him. I had a better plan. I simply sat on top of the gate watching and waiting for the deputy that I had called just minutes earlier. Upon the deputy's arrival, I met him at his car, explained the situation, and revealed my plan to put this all to an end. Returning to the gate, I got down on one knee close to the ground and did my best imitation of a barking dog. I then climbed to the top of the gate and shouted, "Give up now, or we are releasing the dog!"

It worked like a charm. Less than fifty yards in front of me, the guy popped up like a jack-in-the-box. He shouted, "Ok, ok, I'm done, don't do it!" I ordered him to walk to the gate and he complied. It was all over and I'm sure he felt like a dumbass when he realized there was no dog, but one savvy game warden. You can't make these things up.

SPY IN THE SKY

GAME WARDENS FREQUENTLY GET "TIPS." Some pan out, some don't. This one definitely did. Warden Chris Fried called me to tell me about some information he had received from a fisherman concerning some weird activity he had observed on the Cooper Lake Wildlife Management Area. Seems the fisherman had encountered a guy cutting down trees with an axe along the banks of the Middle Sulphur River. As soon as he heard this, Chris knew what was probably going on. As soon as Chris told me the story, I had the exact same thoughts. Somebody was getting ready to set up a marijuana growing operation.

The next morning, Chris and I met at the Highway 1565 bridge that crossed over the river. We launched our small kayaks and headed east. The fisherman with the original tip had told us to look for several freshly cut trees on the south bank. We paddled slowly and used the current to take us about a mile downstream. As we moved along, we were silent, looking and listening. Just after a slight bend in the river, Chris spotted it. A pin oak tree on the bank had been hacked off about waist high.

We beached the kayaks and got out, still looking and listening for any clues. We noticed that someone, using green paint, had covered the top of the stump that was left after the tree was cut. This was an obvious attempt to camouflage the area from anyone who might wander by. Numerous other trees were visible that had been cut and painted in the same manner. We knew now we were in the right spot. We decided Chris would stay with the boats and cover our rear as I climbed the steep riverbank and had a look around.

As I came up over the riverbank, I immediately saw two large, red gas cans and a white trash bag filled with unknown contents. I fell to my hands and knees and drew my pistol. After not seeing any movement, I began to crawl forward. After passing by a hammock hanging between two trees, I found what we were looking for. Hundreds of six-inch marijuana plants in small plastic cups were gathered together, ready to be transplanted. The small plants were all covered in burlap. I had seen this exact thing before years earlier. It was obvious I was in the middle of someone's large-scale operation. I knew from previous experience that, whoever these people were, they were probably armed to the teeth. I had no plans to take them on with a pistol.

I backed out and slid down the riverbank. After giving Chris a brief description of what I had seen, we got the hell out of Dodge. As soon as we were back at the trucks, Chris was on the phone with our captain. We were told not to take any further action until the information was sent up the chain of command. That was fine with us. These guys weren't going anywhere, they were just getting started. Over the next few days, Chris and I bounced some plans off each other. We were just happy with the knowledge that some drug kingpin was about to be in for one hell of a surprise.

One week later, our district had a scheduled meeting at a ranch. All the wardens in the district were there, including our captain and major. After taking care of district business, the captain pulled Chris and me aside and said the major wanted to talk to us about the situation going on at the river. We both figured we were about to be told to put together a plan and a date for a raid. We were wrong. We were actually told that we were to stand down and the department "scout" team would be handling things from that point.

To say I was pissed would have been an understatement. I objected and wanted to know why we were being pushed out of a situation in our own district. Basically, it was insinuated the scout team was better trained and better equipped. Horseshit if I ever heard it. The notion that anyone in the entire department was better trained, more physically able, and better equipped to handle the takedown of this specific dope-grow at the river was nonsense. I was overruled and we accepted the orders from above. There was one slight problem, though. Chris and I were the only ones who knew where the grow was at and a red X on some map wasn't going to cut it. Anyone going to this hidden spot was going to need a guide.

I figured we were now out of the loop so I shrugged off the whole matter and went about my usual business. A month passed. Then one day my phone rang. A game warden with our department scout team was on the other end.

"Hey, Benny, would you be able to meet me at Majors Field in Greenville and go for a plane ride?"

"Yes…. What time?"

"Can you possibly meet us in one hour?"

"I'll be there."

I knew this had something to do with what we had found at the river. I was told a white twin-engine prop plane would land and I was to walk out on the runway and to board it. Sixty minutes later and right on time, a white plane with no markings at all landed and taxied up near the small terminal. The side door opened and a ramp lowered. I was there waiting. I climbed the steps and boarded the plane. I was amazed. This was no ordinary plane. Behind the pilot and copilot there were no seats, only electronics…lots of electronics that took up most of the space in the cabin. I was told to go to the rear of the plane. At the back, I sat down in a small seat attached to the wall and strapped myself in. On the other side of the plane, a man sat in front of several large computer screens. Through headphones, I was able to converse with everyone inside the plane. We took off and, just as I figured we would, headed toward Cooper Lake.

During the nine-minute flight, I was asked to help locate and point out the area where the grow operation was situated. Once we arrived over the river, very powerful cameras mounted in the plane showed us a close-up and detailed view of the ground below. We began to circle. Even at ten thousand feet above, objects on the ground could be seen through the dense canopy of treetops. After a couple of passes, I was able to pick out the gas cans and white trash bag that I had previously seen. They had not been moved. Pointing at one of the screens I said, "That's it…. That's the spot right there."

The man seated behind all the electronics moved a cursor on the screen over to the now-visible gas cans and locked it on the target below. I then heard the pilot say to him, "I'm turning the aircraft over to you." The plane went into tight circles and the entire area was photographed and mapped from above.

We landed back in Greenville in less than thirty minutes. As I exited the plane, I turned to take one last look. I thought to myself, "So, that's what a government spy plane looks like…. Wow!" So now it was obvious that something was about to go down in regards to the grow operation at the Middle Sulphur River. However, as is so often the case, Mother Nature had other plans. Over the next several days, it began to rain. It continued to rain. It rained for a solid week, off and on. Over twelve inches fell in all. The rain caused a flood on the Middle Sulphur River like I had not seen in my lifetime. The water was three feet deep over the highway at the bridge. It was probably five feet deep over the grow operation. Anything downstream of the bridge would have been swept away.

After the rain finally stopped and the water receded, the captain called. Chris and I finally got our way, after all. Or, at least, in a way we did. The captain said he was sending us two scout wardens and we were to return to the grow operation to see if it was still there. The next morning we did just that. Four wardens went in, using kayaks. We discovered it was all gone. Everything had been washed away for the most part, and the area was abandoned. I was personally disappointed. I wanted a chance to round up these fools. It wouldn't be too long before I got another chance.

Summer came to a close. In September, hunting seasons began to open in Texas. It was a Saturday when the special hog hunting season opened on the Cooper Lake Management Area. Hunters were also pursuing doves and ducks. The woods were full of hunters when the sun came up that morning. I was still eating breakfast when Chris called, almost breathless, and said, "Hey, get your stuff and meet me on Highway 71 in Horton."

"What's going on?"

"I don't have time to explain, but our dope growers are back."

I grabbed my keys and ran out of the house. On the way to Horton, I was able to get Chris back on the phone and get more information. Chris had gotten a call from a ranger at the state park, who advised hunters had come into the lobby there to report a bunch of marijuana being grown in the woods. The hunters also stated they had encountered four to five men living in tents. Chris had spoken with one of the hunters by phone and arranged to meet them so they could show us where we needed to go. I met Chris and Game Warden Jarod Bryant in the gravel parking lot at the public hunting area just off Highway 71. As we waited for the hunters to arrive, we all geared up. M4 rifles were readied, along with extra ammo and tactical vests. I was worried that, since they had been alerted, the bad guys would be fleeing soon if they had not already. When the hunters showed back up, we interviewed them again to get all the information we could about what we were walking into. One brave hunter volunteered to lead us to the men living in tents.

"Should I carry a gun with me?"

"You're damn right you should carry a gun."

"What if they are there?"

"If they are there, you don't do anything, just leave and make a phone call. We will take it from there."

With those words, four of us climbed the gate and entered the woods. We followed closely behind the hunter as he led us down a narrow trail for about four hundred yards. Suddenly, he dropped to one knee and pointed to a levee. Four tents could plainly be seen sitting on top of the levee. I thanked the man for his help and sent him away. Once he was out of sight, Chris, Jarod, and I huddled. It was decided Jarod would cover us from behind a large tree. Chris went right and I went left. Slowly and carefully we flanked the tents. They were empty. Everyone had already gone. Standing on top of the levee, Chris and I looked out over several acres of standing marijuana, six feet tall. I now found myself in a familiar situation. We got the dope, but they got away. Our department brought in a helicopter and the local prison brought in tracking dogs, but it was a waste of time. These guys were long gone.

In the end, we recovered a lot of equipment, including water pumps and generators. We also cut down seven thousand plants. A large pit was dug into the ground. All the plants were thrown into the pit, burned using diesel fuel, then buried. Looking back on that whole ordeal, it became obvious what had transpired over five months. A huge grow operation was set up by four to five men. The floods came and washed it all away. Rather than give up and leave, the bad guys simply moved to another spot nearby and started over. In the end, I'm not sure whether we won or lost. Yes, we shut down a huge operation and got their dope...but we spent a lot of valuable time and resources doing so. No doubt they would be back for another try, at another place, at another time.

Rock-Solid Guarantee

IT WAS LUNCHTIME and I was sitting in my truck in Commerce, Texas, finishing up a burger at a Sonic Drive-In, when my old bag phone began to ring. Peeling back the Velcro cover, I grabbed the receiver and answered the call.

"Hello, State Game Warden." It was a familiar voice on the other end, seventy-five-year-old rancher Everitt Sloan.

"Benny, I got a problem. There is a man hunting with dogs on my property and he won't leave. They have already ran my cows through the fence."

"Have you already spoken to the man?"

"Yes, I have.... I told him to get off but he just started cussing me."

"Do you have any idea who he is?"

"Yes, I do.... Roy Friddle."

When I heard that name, I could feel my blood pressure rise. Old man Sloan went on to explain that after seeing his cattle running, he went to investigate and found a pack of dogs wearing orange collars that had a hog bayed in his hay meadow. When a man came walking out of a grove of nearby trees, he confronted him. After recognizing him, the old rancher reminded Friddle that he had been told several times before to stay off the property without permission. Friddle then began cussing the old man and told him to mind his own business. While I listened to Mr. Sloan's story, I realized his voice was cracking and it sounded like he was in tears. My blood pressure went up even further.

"Mr. Sloan, I am on my way. Do you want to prosecute him if I find him?"

"Yes, I do!"

I hung up the phone and dialed my partner at the time, Hopkins County warden Sean Reneau, who was nearby. After explaining the situation to Sean, I asked him to meet me at the 904 bridge near Pecan Gap. The 904 bridge crossed over the North Sulphur River. When I arrived, I spotted a pickup truck parked beside the bridge. I ran the plates and just as I thought it would, the registration came back to Friddle. At this point, he was caught. It was just a matter of finding him. Sean pulled up just as I was unloading the four-wheeled ATV out of my truck. A set of ramps leaned against his tailgate told me Friddle was on a four-wheeler as well. Sean and I loaded onto my ATV and followed tracks down into the riverbed, where we headed east toward Mr. Sloan's property about a mile away. The North Sulphur riverbed is very wide and flat and usually dry most of the year. Navigating the gravel bars wasn't much different than driving down a country road.

The man we were looking for was a poor excuse for a human. He was a loathsome individual that I had arrested several times in the past. Over the years, almost every game warden in Northeast Texas had dealings with him. He definitely earned the title "poacher." I had no use for Friddle and I was aware the feeling was mutual.

After only a few minutes in the riverbed, I saw an ATV pulling a small trailer approaching us. When we met head-to-head, I motioned for the driver to stop. It was Friddle. He was pulling a small trailer full of dogs, all wearing orange collars. I had hoped to catch him on Mr. Sloan's property but there was absolutely no doubt he was the man we were looking for. After dismounting, Sean and I walked over to Friddle and I told him to turn his machine off. He immediately started his usual crap. He demanded to know why we were stopping him. I explained he was suspected of trespassing and again told him to kill the engine and get off. He began to curse and complain of harassment. He did eventually get off of the ATV. Knowing Friddle was a convicted felon, I searched him and his machine for firearms, which, of course, caused him to complain even more. His bitching then started to get personal.

After finding no weapons, except for the big knife strapped to his hip, I began to question him about his conversation with the old landowner. He played dumb as a stump. He denied ever having any conversations with Mr. Sloan on that day or any other day. He said, "That old man is a lying son of a bitch. I never set foot on that fool's place."

Those words coming out of his mouth flipped a switch in my head. I recalled my earlier phone call with old Mr. Sloan and hearing the emotion in his voice as he tearfully asked me for help. I had had enough. I turned and began walking to my ATV. I began to take off my gun belt as I walked. I laid the gun belt across the seat and then removed my badge and ballpoint pen from my uniform shirt. By this time Sean had caught up to me.

"Benny, what are you doing?"

"I'm about to beat the living hell out of Roy Friddle."

"No, I'm not gonna let you do it."

"He has had this coming for a long time and today is the day."

"I'm telling you, he ain't worth it."

I paused long enough to think about it. I stepped around Sean and said, "What's it gonna be, Friddle?"

Upon hearing this, he just sat down on the ground and crossed his arms across his chest. After putting my equipment back on and in place, I instructed Friddle to follow us to the trucks. The short ride back to the truck gave me time to calm down and collect my thoughts. After the ATVs were loaded back onto the trucks, I used a disposable camera to take pictures of Friddle and the dogs in the trailer. I then explained that we were going to continue our investigation and would be back in touch very soon. He was about to leave when I said to him, "One more thing, Friddle.... Take off your boots."

"What do you mean, take off my boots?"

"I mean just what I said.... Take them off.... They are evidence now."

I was not going to take any chances. I knew Mr. Sloan had positively identified him and the dogs but it was one's word against the other. After Friddle left, I contacted Mr. Sloan at his home and got a written statement. He then led me down to his hay meadow where we found a dead hog with its throat cut. Nearby I found what I was really looking for. Fresh footprints in the soft dirt that perfectly matched the tread pattern of the boots taken from my suspect's feet. More photos were taken. That's all I needed. Later that week, a warrant was issued for Friddle's arrest. He was charged with hunting without landowner consent and hunting without a valid license. He turned himself in at the jail in Cooper.

Fast-forward five months.

Friddle pled not guilty and demanded a trial. He got his wish. On the morning the trial was scheduled to begin, I arrived at the courthouse early. Many people were at the courthouse that had received jury summons. I met with the county attorney in a conference room just outside the courtroom. He advised that jury selection would take most of the morning so I wouldn't be needed until after lunch. I was told if things changed, I would be notified.

I patrolled the shoreline of Cooper Lake for a couple of hours and then had lunch with a couple of landowners on the square in town. After lunch, I waited in my office in the basement in the courthouse. Around two o'clock, my pager buzzed. It displayed the county attorney's phone number. I figured I was needed upstairs. At the top of the stairs, I noticed the courtroom was empty. At that very moment, Friddle's two attorneys and the county attorney walked out if the courtroom. Pointing his finger my way, Friddle's lead attorney said, "Well there he is, right there."

I took this to mean I had been the topic of some conversation. The county attorney motioned for me to follow them onto the elevator. On the way down, he told me Friddle had been convinced to wisely take a plea agreement. His attorney chimed in, saying, "We could have put this to rest a long time ago, but Roy was dead set on testifying."

I just shrugged my shoulders as the doors opened and we stepped out into the hallway. The attorney continued, saying, "Yeah, Roy wanted a jury to hear his story. He claimed you threatened to beat the hell out of him."

There was a moment of silence as I thought about it for half a second and replied, "That, sir, was no threat.... It was a rock-solid guarantee." I placed my cowboy hat on my head, turned my back on the men, and walked out of the courthouse.

A Hole in One

THE SECOND HALF OF OCTOBER is generally a slow time for a game warden in Dallam County. After the close of the antelope season in the first week of October, there just isn't much going on. Because there is no water, there are no fish. The doves have all migrated south. The duck and goose season, along with pheasant season, is still weeks away. There are no squirrels or turkeys to hunt. About the only thing you can hunt legally during this time is deer, with archery equipment.

Hunting deer with a bow in the far northwest corner of the Texas Panhandle is a tough proposition. The area around Dalhart is either flat, open prairie or cropland totally void of any trees. Without any place to hang a tree stand, getting close enough to a deer for a shot with an arrow was very difficult, but not totally impossible. In the two years that I worked Dallam and Hartley Counties, I knew of a few deer that were taken with a bow but I never actually checked one in the field.

One morning while on my way to Texline, I decided to stop by the meat locker and visit my friend Ed, who ran the operation. When I stepped inside the office, no one was around so I went back to the big walk-in cooler in the back. I expected to find maybe an antelope or two hanging and maybe a couple of elk from Colorado, but not much else. Walking into the cooler, the only carcass hanging was the skinned body of a

109

huge mule deer. I was checking the deer out, unconcerned, until Ed's son walked into the cooler.

"That's a big deer, ain't it?"

I replied, "It sure is.... Where did it come from?"

"Somewhere around Dalhart."

"Dalhart?"

Now I was concerned. If someone had killed this deer legally around Dalhart, it had to have been taken with a bow and arrow. Being a naturally suspicious game warden, I thought the chances of that were not real high. I now began to examine the deer a little closer and noticed two interesting things. First, the deer's neck had been severed and removed right at the base of the shoulders. Usually Ed's crew left at least ten inches of the neck that could be boned out for stew or chili meat. The other thing was the wound in the animal's shoulder. I could clearly see the familiar X cut made by a broadhead. But absent from the entry point was the hemorrhaging and severe discoloration that would be expected. Pulling apart the ribs I peered inside the chest cavity. I came to an obvious conclusion that the arrow that caused the wound was shot into the deer postmortem.

"Who killed this deer?" I asked.

"Randall Fritz brought it in."

"Did he bring it in hide on or hide off?"

"He brought it in already skinned this morning."

This turned out to be another clue. Most hunters brought their deer to the meat locker with the hide on and let Ed and his skinners remove it, since it was included in the processing fee anyway. I retrieved Fritz's deer tag and found it to be properly filled out. Ed came in about this time and asked me if there was a problem with the deer. I explained to him that I had some questions for the hunter but he was OK to process the animal as usual.

I headed back to Dalhart to locate Randall, known as "Randy" to his friends. On the way, I checked our department records and found an address for Randy on Peach Street in Dalhart. It took me twenty-five minutes to make the drive back to town, and in that time, I was able to come up with a cell phone number for him.

I arrived at the small frame house to find no one home. As I was standing on the porch knocking on the door, I noticed a dog chewing on something in the front yard. It turned out to be a deer's leg. I knew now that I was at the right place. Falling back on game warden experience and a strong hunch, I decided to try something. The house across the street was vacant. I backed my truck into the vacant garage next to the run-down house. I then dialed Randy's phone number. He answered the phone cheerfully, saying, "Yellllo."

As soon as I told him who was on the other end of the line, I sensed a change in his voice. After each question, he seemed to become a little more nervous. At this point, I told a little white lie. I told him I was in Texline, thirty-eight miles away. I went onto ask directions to his house and explained that I needed to meet him there in one hour to discuss the deer. He said he was at work but agreed to meet in one hour. I hung up the phone and leaned my seat back. It didn't take very long.

I hadn't even gotten comfortable before a truck came roaring down the street and pulled up in the yard at Randy's house. A man got out at a full sprint and ran around behind the house. About thirty seconds passed before the same man, that turned out to be Randy, came running back around the house carrying a huge set of antlers. He ran around the truck and tossed them in the back. I started my truck and pulled out onto the street. Upon seeing me, Randy walked to the front porch and sat down.

I pulled up in the yard alongside his work truck and got out. I greeted him at his porch by saying, "I got here a little sooner than expected, I hope you don't mind." Looking down at the ground, he just nodded his head.

He spent the next five minutes explaining to me how and where he had killed his twenty-seven-inch wide, twelve-point trophy buck with a recurve bow. I just listened and tried to keep an open mind just in case I was totally wrong about this whole matter. After listening to his story, I asked to see the cape from the deer. He first said he had dumped the whole hide in a ditch outside of town. What Randy didn't know was that I had done a little more digging over the phone on my way from Texline to Dalhart. Someone I had talked to told me Randy was an aspiring taxidermist in training.

"You killed the deer of a lifetime and you're not going to mount it?" I continued to question. "That's hard to believe.... Why not?"

He stood silently for a moment and then confessed to having the cape inside a freezer inside his house.

"Why did you just lie to me?"

"I'm sorry.... It's just that I'm real nervous."

I followed him inside to his kitchen. Along the way through the house, I saw several nice sets of mule deer antlers lying around. He pulled a black garbage bag out of his freezer and handed it to me. I walked back outside to my patrol truck and lowered the tailgate. I pulled the partially frozen cape out and rolled it flat. On one side, I found a nasty jagged hole about the size of a golf ball. On the other side, midway down the neck, I found a small, perfectly round hole about the diameter of a pencil. Now, there was no doubt what had happened.

I looked up at him and asked, "Well, Randy, what about these strange holes?"

He looked me right in the eyes and tried to tell me he had only wounded the deer with his bow, and then retrieved a .270 rifle in order to put the deer out of his suffering.

"You better try again Randy.... This ain't no fool you're talking to."

After a long pause, he threw up his hands and said, "Okay, you caught me." He confessed to shooting the deer out the window of his work truck while he was checking natural gas wells. He insisted that he shot it on a ranch where he legitimately had permission to hunt.

I was certain he did not kill the big muley where he said he did; however, I couldn't prove otherwise. A further investigation into the matter revealed that several of his coworkers at the gas company routinely carried rifles in their company work trucks in an attempt to pull off a drive-by similar to what Randy had done. The company officials were none too happy when I explained to them what had been going on. In the end, the big mule deer was seized and Randy's Christmas budget was a little thin for a couple of years.

So You Want to Be a Game Warden?

I WISH I HAD A DOLLAR BILL for every time I heard someone tell me they wanted to be a game warden. Others were more descriptive. They "dreamed" of becoming a game warden. So many times after these conversations, I wondered if some of these folks had even the slightest clue what they were asking for. The old saying "Be careful what you wish for, you just might get it" is very true. So you think you want to be a game warden? Allow me to pass along some valuable information so anyone considering this career choice can make an informed decision.

First, I will say that anyone can put on a uniform, call themselves anything they like, do just enough to fly under the radar, and collect a check at the end of the month. To be an outstanding officer, you have to live it. I've said it before: being a game warden is not a job, it's a way of life. That's not limited to Texas. Warden work is warden work whether you are in Alaska, or Florida, or anywhere in between.

What are your motives for becoming a warden? So you can protect the animals from being killed? I hear this lot. Please be aware that, as a game warden, you will work for an agency that supports and encourages the legal harvest of birds, fish, and mammals of many types. You will get the opportunity to prevent the illegal harm to animal life, but you must be there to assist and manage legal hunters and their activities. Over the years, you will check thousands of dead birds and animals! If you are antihunting, there is no place for you.

On the other end of the spectrum, there may be those who say they want to be a warden because "I love to hunt and fish." So what? Is that a qualification? It is true that game wardens usually have access to great hunting and fishing opportunities. But remember, you are not hired to become a professional hunter or fisherman. That truck and boat you use are not yours. They belong to the taxpayers. The same taxpayers want you to earn your salary by working the required hours. It might be hard to do that sitting in a duck blind every day of the week.... "Just saying."

Do you like your weekends? Say goodbye to them. Think about it: Saturdays and Sundays are when the vast majority of outdoor recreation takes place. In the spring and summer, you will be expected to spend your weekends patrolling on the water. In the fall and winter, your weekends will be in that patrol truck burning up back roads.

Looking for a nine-to-five job? Look somewhere else. You will be on call twenty-four hours a day for emergencies. An effective, dependable warden will make himself or herself available to the public and other agencies if needed at all hours. OK, imagine this scenario. You are just about to graduate from the academy. A captain walks into your room and hands you an envelope that contains your first duty assignment. You open it to find that you, your wife, and the kids are relocating to some town you never heard of on the Rio Grande River, halfway between McAllen and Del Rio. Those dreams you had of patrolling sandy beaches at Galveston Island just disappeared.

You do remember that part of the application process where you agreed to accept assignment anywhere in the state? It's real. The good news is that if you go do your job, you can transfer to a place more to your liking in a reasonable amount of time.

Not even fazed? Here's another scene. You hear a shot in the night. You go to investigate and find two heavily intoxicated men standing over a dead deer lying beside a county road. The closest backup officer is twenty minutes away. The two men are holding rifles and are less than cooperative. What are you going to do? Do you possess the backbone to arrest them? Would you have the courage to disarm them? If the answer is no, do yourself a favor and pick a career that is less dangerous. You may be thinking, "Well, I can avoid all that by just not working after the sun goes down." Again, I would say go do something else.

Folks, there will be days when you are shivering and cold and your legs are covered in mud up to your knees. There will be other days when you are hot and sweating and your arms are covered in fish scales up to your elbows. There are hurricanes (Katrina 2005), tornadoes (Canton 2017), mass shootings (Dallas 2019), explosions (West 2013), and every other kind of calamity. You will get a front seat to all of it.

I hope no one misunderstands me. I don't want to discourage anyone from their dreams. I don't want to be a pessimist. But these are things to consider before pursuing this career choice. Being a game warden is a law enforcement position and it is serious business. Now, let me tell you what awaits those who clear the hurdles, graduate the academy, and wear the blue badge. The best, most fulfilling career on earth, in my opinion. The title of game warden is pursued by many but enjoyed by few. In Texas, game wardens have an almost mythical stature. That kind of support was earned by those men and women who came before. If you are going to join that elite group, do it for the right reasons and don't do it half-heartedly. You will get out of it what you put into it.

To those new wardens hitting the field, I would offer this advice. Pour yourself into your work and make it your passion. Never stop learning. Try to become as knowledgeable as possible. Become part of your community. Be proud and brave. Make sure your heart is in the right place and never apologize for doing your job. Make every day count. Do these things and you will have self-satisfaction and be rewarded when it is all said and done.

Speaking of when it's all said and done, how will you know if you made a difference? Let me be clear. The measure is not how many citations you wrote. It's not how many arrests you made. It's definitely not how highly you were promoted. It's your reputation and it is measured by this. If, twenty years after you retire, hunters are still mentioning your name around campfires...then you did your job in a way that made a difference. Using that standard, I am confident my name will not be forgotten.

GOD BLESS TEXAS!

THE END